Responsive Web Design by Example

Embrace responsive design with HTML5, CSS3, JavaScript, jQuery, and Bootstrap 4

Frahaan Hussain

BIRMINGHAM - MUMBAI

Responsive Web Design by Example

First published: December 2017

Production reference: 1061217

Published by Packt Publishing Ltd.
Livery Place
35 Livery Street
Birmingham
B3 2PB, UK.

ISBN 978-1-78728-706-8

www.packtpub.com

Credits

Author
Frahaan Hussain

Reviewer
Sasan Seydnejad

Commissioning Editor
Ashwin Nair

Acquisition Editor
Larissa Pinto

Content Development Editor
Onkar Wani

Technical Editor
Murtaza Tinwala

Copy Editor
Safis Editing

Project Coordinator
Devanshi Doshi

Proofreader
Safis Editing

Indexer
Francy Puthiry

Graphics
Jason Monteiro

Production Coordinator
Arvindkumar Gupta

About the Author

Frahaan Hussain is a young programmer who contributes to the community in many ways, this book being the latest. He runs his own company, Sonar Systems, which is a world leader in online educational content. Sonar Systems has created many open source frameworks including Cocos Helper and PHP Web Framework to assist developers worldwide. Plus the company specializes in game development as well as app publishing. He has a degree in computer games programming and has developed many websites for a wide range of clients, making him fully aware of the development lifecycle and the practical needs of the developer. He has worked for Accenture, which is the world's largest consultancy firm.

About the Reviewer

Sasan Seydnejad has more than a decade of experience in web UI and frontend application development using JavaScript, CSS, and HTML in .NET and ASP.NET environments. He specializes in modular SPA design and implementation, responsive mobile-friendly user interfaces, AJAX, client architecture, and UX design using HTML5, CSS3, and their related technologies. He implements framework-less and framework-based applications using Node.js, MongoDB, Express.js, and Angular. He's also the author of the book *Modular Programming with JavaScript*, Packt.

www.PacktPub.com

For support files and downloads related to your book, please visit www.PacktPub.com.

Did you know that Packt offers eBook versions of every book published, with PDF and ePub files available? You can upgrade to the eBook version at www.PacktPub.com and as a print book customer, you are entitled to a discount on the eBook copy. Get in touch with us at service@packtpub.com for more details.

At www.PacktPub.com, you can also read a collection of free technical articles, sign up for a range of free newsletters and receive exclusive discounts and offers on Packt books and eBooks.

https://www.packtpub.com/mapt

Get the most in-demand software skills with Mapt. Mapt gives you full access to all Packt books and video courses, as well as industry-leading tools to help you plan your personal development and advance your career.

Why subscribe?

- Fully searchable across every book published by Packt
- Copy and paste, print, and bookmark content
- On demand and accessible via a web browser

Customer Feedback

Thanks for purchasing this Packt book. At Packt, quality is at the heart of our editorial process. To help us improve, please leave us an honest review on this book's Amazon page at https://www.amazon.com/dp/B077T1FW6R.

If you'd like to join our team of regular reviewers, you can e-mail us at customerreviews@packtpub.com. We award our regular reviewers with free eBooks and videos in exchange for their valuable feedback. Help us be relentless in improving our products!

Table of Contents

Preface   1

Chapter 1: What is Responsive Web Design?   7

Responsive design philosophy   8
Responsive design principles   9
Responsive versus adaptive   9
Breakpoints   10
Relative units   11
Maximum and minimum values   11
Nested objects   12
Mobile or desktop first   12
Bitmaps versus vectors   13
Responsive grids and columns   14
Summary   16

Chapter 2: What is Bootstrap, Why Do We Use It?   17

Brief history of Bootstrap   17
Why use Bootstrap?   18
Why Bootstrap?   19
Bootstrap's grid system   20
Basics   21
Usage and examples   22
Equal width columns example   23
Multi-row, equal-width columns example   24
Multi-row, equal-width columns without multiple rows example   25
Differently sized columns   25
Differently sized columns with screen size restrictions   26
Mixing and matching   27
Vertical alignment   30
Horizontal alignment   32
Column offsetting   33
Grid wrap up   34
Bootstrap components   34
Summary   35

Chapter 3: Reusable Project Template   37

What is a reusable project template?   37
Development environment prerequisites   41

Creating our reusable project template   42
Simple Bootstrap example   42
Abstraction   44
Extending the header   46
Extending the footer   48
Extending the main body   51
Troubleshooting   52
PHP errors   52
CSS not applying   52
Summary   52
Chapter 4: Creating the Introduction Section   53
What is a single-page website?   53
Single-page examples   54
Android KitKat promotional homepage   54
GoldSquare   55
Anthony Designer   56
Richman   57
Implementing our introduction section   57
What is a jumbotron?   57
Implementing a basic jumbotron   59
Adding an image to the jumbotron   61
Combining text and images in a jumbotron   66
Anchoring a section to the navigation bar   70
Animating our navigation bar anchor   72
Fixing footer visibility and the location problem   77
Placing the header on top   78
Changing the current button selected   80
Common pitfalls   82
Navigation bar height variance on mobile devices   82
Navigation bar button anchoring   82
Summary   83
Chapter 5: Creating a Generic Reusable Single Page Section   85
Different sections in single page websites   85
Single page section examples   86
Contact form   86
About us   88
Projects/work   89
Opening times   90
Implementing our generic reusable single page section   90
What will the Our Team section contain?   91

Creating the Our Team section container   92
Anchoring the Team section to the navigation bar   93
Adding the team's pictures   95
Team member info text   105
Team member social links   107
Summary   110
Chapter 6: Creating a Contact Us Section   111
Contact Us examples for single page websites   111
Richman   112
Bueno   113
This also   114
Design museum   115
Choice screening   116
Implementing the Contact Us section   117
What will the Contact Us section contain?   117
Creating the Contact Us section container   117
Anchoring the Contact Us section to the navigation bar   120
Adding the contact form   121
Summary   127
Chapter 7: Creating the Blog Posts Home Page   129
Blog examples   129
TechCrunch   130
Gawker   131
Microsoft News   132
Johnny Cupcakes   133
TESCO Living   134
Setting up the base project   135
Removing all unnecessary files   135
Refactoring the index.css file   135
Refactoring the index.php file   136
Refactoring the HEADER.php snippet file   136
Refactoring the index.js file   137
What will our blog home page look like?   138
Implementing the blog home page section   138
Implementing the image slider   138
Simple image slider   138
Adding back and forward buttons to the slider   143
Carousel indicators   146
Captioning our carousel   149

Implementing the blog posts	150
Adding cards	152
Summary	158
Chapter 8: Creating the Blog Posts Page	159
Blog post page examples	159
TechCrunch	160
Gawker	161
Microsoft News	162
Johnny Cupcakes	163
Tesco Living	164
What will our blog post page consist of?	165
What does the post content consist of?	165
What does the popular and recommended sidebar consists of?	166
Implementing the blog post page	166
Implementing the post's main content	167
Adding the blog post title and banner image	167
Adding the snapshot paragraph	170
Adding the body	172
More useful links	177
Implementing the sidebar	179
Further extending the blog	186
Summary	186
Chapter 9: Adding a Sidebar to the Social Network	187
Social network sidebar examples	187
Facebook	188
Google+	189
YouTube	190
Minds	191
Myspace	192
What will our social network sidebar consist of?	193
Implementing the sidebar	193
Implementing the burger button	193
Implementing the sidebar HTML side	196
Implementing the sidebar CSS side	198
Summary	204
Chapter 10: Creating the Home page in Our Social Network	205
Social network timeline examples	205
Facebook	205
Google+	207

YouTube	208
Twitter	209
Medium	210
What will our social network timeline consist of?	211
Implementing the timeline	211
Implementing the input section	212
Implementing the timeline feed section	213
Adding the user's thumbnail image	216
Adding the user's name/username	218
Adding the post's timestamp	219
Adding the post's main body	220
Going forward and extending the timeline	223
Summary	223
Chapter 11: Creating the User's Profile Page	**225**
Social network profile examples	225
What will our social network user page consist of?	226
Implementing the jumbotron	226
Creating a basic jumbotron with a banner image	227
Adding the overlay text	232
Implementing the small cards	234
Implementing the large cards	237
Summary	239
Chapter 12: Displaying Thumbnails of Our Photos	**241**
Photo gallery home page examples	241
Pinterest	242
9GAG	243
Google Photos	244
GIPHY	245
Vent	246
What will our photo gallery home page consist of?	247
Implementing the thumbnails	247
Adding the home page title	247
Adding the picture thumbnails	248
Adding pagination	251
Summary	254
Chapter 13: Opening Images Using a Light Box	**255**
Light box examples	255
Pinterest	256

Google Photos   257
Dan Kennedy   258
Salter   259
Arild Danielsen Photographer   260
What will our light box consist of?   261
Implementing the light box   261
Adding a simple modal   261
Adding an image to the modal   266
Making the modal content appear dynamically   269
Summary   271
Index   273

Preface

Responsive Web Design by Example is your quick and easy guide to learning how to incorporate responsiveness into your website's design and creation. This book uses the concept of creating a varied array of websites to teach you the essentials and fundamentals of responsive web design. While also teaching about good practices for web design and development in general. This book will teach you this using the common web technologies HTML, CSS, and JavaScript, while also leveraging the immensely popular responsive framework Bootstrap.

This book aims to be your one stop for all things responsive and Bootstrap in web design and development. I have also created a popular YouTube channel which provides free educational videos, including on web development, to further assist you on your development journey:

```
https://www.youtube.com/user/sonarsystemslimited
```

Who this book is for

If you are a web developer interested in incorporating responsive web design into your websites, then this book is for you. Familiarity with HTML5, CSS3, and command lines, though not essential, will be a great help in getting the most out of this book.

What this book covers

Chapter 1, *What Is Responsive Web Design?*, explains the basics of responsiveness in web design and its importance to the internet.

Chapter 2, *What Is Bootstrap, Why We Use It?*, explains what the Bootstrap framework is and how it ties into the world of responsive web design and development.

Chapter 3, *Reusable Project Template*, explains the importance of having a reusable project template and how to create one for all your future projects.

Chapter 4, *Creating the Introduction Section*, shows the creation of the introduction section for the first project.

Chapter 5, *Creating a Generic Reusable Single Page Section*, shows how to create a section that can be reused for different topics.

Chapter 6, *Creating a Contact Us Section*, shows how to create a section that will enable the user to communicate with the website's creators.

Chapter 7, *Creating the Blog Posts Homepage*, begins the second project in this book.

Chapter 8, *Creating the Blog Posts Page*, covers creating a page to display the blog post in its full glory.

Chapter 9, *Adding a Sidebar to the Social Network*, shows how a sidebar can be implemented and used to enhance your website.

Chapter 10, *Creating the Homepage in Our Social Network*, implements the home page of our social network to display social posts.

Chapter 11, *Creating the User's Profile Page*, adds a page to display users, profile data.

Chapter 12, *Displaying Thumbnails of Our Photos*, starts our final project, creating a photo gallery.

Chapter 13, *Opening Images Using a Light Box*, shows how to open the images using a light box to focus on a particular image.

To get the most out of this book

You will need a computer with access to the internet, a web browser and local web server for testing, and your favorite IDE/text editor for coding the projects in.

Download the example code files

You can download the example code files for this book from your account at http://www.packtpub.com. If you purchased this book elsewhere, you can visit http://www.packtpub.com/support and register to have the files emailed directly to you.

You can download the code files by following these steps:

1. Log in or register at http://www.packtpub.com.
2. Select the **SUPPORT** tab.
3. Click on **Code Downloads & Errata**.
4. Enter the name of the book in the **Search** box and follow the on-screen instructions.

Once the file is downloaded, please make sure that you unzip or extract the folder using the latest version of:

- WinRAR / 7-Zip for Windows
- Zipeg / iZip / UnRarX for Mac
- 7-Zip / PeaZip for Linux

The code bundle for the book is also hosted on GitHub at `https://github.com/PacktPublishing/Responsive-Web-Design-by-Example-Third-Edition`. We also have other code bundles from our rich catalog of books and videos available at `https://github.com/PacktPublishing/`. Check them out!

Conventions used

There are a number of text conventions used throughout this book.

`CodeInText`: Indicates code words in text, database table names, folder names, filenames, file extensions, pathnames, dummy URLs, user input, and Twitter handles. Here is an example: "Common bitmap formats include `.png` and `.jpg`."

Bold: Indicates a new term, an important word, or words that you see on the screen, for example, in menus or dialog boxes, also appear in the text like this. Here is an example: "I would recommend copying the code from our GitHub page, as the CSS and JavaScript files are stored on a **Content Delivery Network (CDN)**."

Warnings or important notes appear in a box like this.

Tips and tricks appear like this.

Reader feedback

Feedback from our readers is always welcome. Let us know what you think about this book—what you liked or disliked. Reader feedback is important for us as it helps us develop titles that you will really get the most out of.

To send us general feedback, simply e-mail `feedback@packtpub.com`, and mention the book's title in the subject of your message.

If there is a topic that you have expertise in and you are interested in either writing or contributing to a book, see our author guide at `www.packtpub.com/authors`.

Customer support

Now that you are the proud owner of a Packt book, we have a number of things to help you to get the most from your purchase.

Errata

Although we have taken every care to ensure the accuracy of our content, mistakes do happen. If you find a mistake in one of our books—maybe a mistake in the text or the code—we would be grateful if you could report this to us. By doing so, you can save other readers from frustration and help us improve subsequent versions of this book. If you find any errata, please report them by visiting `http://www.packtpub.com/submit-errata`, selecting your book, clicking on the Errata Submission Form link, and entering the details of your errata. Once your errata are verified, your submission will be accepted and the errata will be uploaded to our website or added to any list of existing errata under the Errata section of that title.

To view the previously submitted errata, go to https://www.packtpub.com/books/content/support and enter the name of the book in the search field. The required information will appear under the Errata section.

Piracy

Piracy of copyrighted material on the Internet is an ongoing problem across all media. At Packt, we take the protection of our copyright and licenses very seriously. If you come across any illegal copies of our works in any form on the Internet, please provide us with the location address or website name immediately so that we can pursue a remedy.

Please contact us at copyright@packtpub.com with a link to the suspected pirated material.

We appreciate your help in protecting our authors and our ability to bring you valuable content.

Questions

If you have a problem with any aspect of this book, you can contact us at questions@packtpub.com, and we will do our best to address the problem.

1
What is Responsive Web Design?

This chapter will explain what Responsive Web Design is, how it benefits our websites, and the core concepts that it consists of.

The topics covered in this chapter are as follows:

- Responsive design philosophy
- Responsive design principles
- Responsive grid and columns
- Smooth user experience
- Understanding responsive grid systems
- Design methodologies
- User-friendly websites
- Elegant mobile experience
- Adaptive design and development

Responsive design philosophy

There was a time when most web surfing occurred on a computer with a standard-sized/ratio monitor. It was more than adequate to create websites with a non responsive layout in mind. But over the last 10 years there has been an exponential boom of new devices in a plethora of form factors, from mobile phones, tablets, watches and a wide range of screen sizes. This growth has created a huge fragmentation problem, so creating websites with a single layout is no longer acceptable. A website with a lot of content that works great on desktops doesn't work very well on a mobile device that has a significantly smaller screen. Such content is unreadable, forcing the user to zoom in and out constantly. One might try making everything bigger so it looks good on mobiles, but then on a desktop, the content doesn't take advantage of the immense real estate offered by bigger screens.

Responsive Web Design is a method that allows the design to respond based on the user's input and environment, and thus based on the size of the screen, the device, and its orientation. This philosophy blends elements of flexible grids and layouts, images, and media queries in CSS.

Enter Responsive Web Design. This alleviates this problem by allowing developers and designers to create websites that adapt to all screen sizes/ratios. There are various approaches that different websites take, but the core concept is illustrated in the following figure:

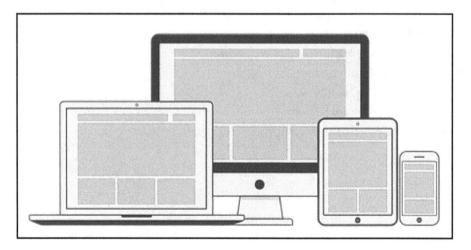

The preceding figure shows how the same website's layout can be adapted to suit different devices. On the desktop there is a lot more real estate, so the content is bigger and more can fit on a single row. But, as the screen size shrinks and its orientation changes, the content readjusts itself to accommodate this change. This provides a seamless and elegant experience for the user on all form factors. If you look closely at the preceding figure and at modern websites, you will see a grid that the content conforms to. The grid is used to lay out the content of a website, and both of these elements go hand in hand. This grid system is one of the most important aspects of how Responsive Web Design works, and this will be covered in depth very soon.

Responsive design principles

This section will cover the main principles behind designing responsive websites. Though these aren't set in stone and will change over time, they will provide a great foundation.

Responsive versus adaptive

Responsive designs constantly change website layouts depending on their size and orientation. A single pixel resize will tend to have an effect on the layout, usually not by a lot.

Adaptive schemes, on the other hand, have preset layouts, which are loaded depending on the size of the screen. This technique doesn't look as fluid and seamless as do responsive designs.

Modern-day Responsive Web Design usually incorporates both methods. Set layouts will be provided, as can be seen in the previous figure. But any changes made to a website's size will have an impact in real time through responsive scaling.

Breakpoints

Breakpoints are points at which a website's layout is no longer fit for the screen size, device, and/or orientation, and we are able to use different and unique layouts to accommodate the various changes that can occur to screens. When these points occur, the current layout is switched for a more suitable layout. For example, a mobile device in portrait mode will not effectively be able to use a layout that is designed for a widescreen desktop display; this just isn't possible. However, by using breakpoints a single website can serve many screen variations whilst making the website feel like it was designed with the user's current screen, device, and/or orientation in mind. This does not occur when reloading the web page, but content moves around dynamically and is scaled accordingly. Without breakpoints the website would appear with the same layout on all form factors and browser sizes, which using the example we just mentioned, would not be fit for purpose.

These breakpoints usually occur when the width of the browser changes and falls into the category of another more appropriate layout.

There are a few fundamentals that should be mentioned regarding the responsive philosophy of Responsive Web Design:

- **Screen resolution**: This is immensely influential in responsive design. The first thought for many designers is to design based on the resolution of the screen. But modern-day phones have resolutions of 1080p and beyond, which for the most part is still the de facto standard for desktops with some exceptions in 4K and ultrawide displays. This would prevent us from fully targeting all devices, as there is so much crossover in resolutions between devices. That is the reason why pixel density is very important when deciding which layout should be used as a 5-inch 1080p mobile display will be cramming the pixels in a lot closer than a 32-inch 1080p display. They both have the same resolution for the mobile device and they have a significantly higher pixel density, which helps distinguish between the device types. The viewport should also be taken into consideration, which is the user's visible area of a web page. This would allow us to rearrange content based on how much content should be displayed.
- **Media queries**: These are amazing facets within CSS that allow us to actually detect changes in a screen such as its size and an event device type. These are the things used to specify code for a specific layout, such as a mobile or desktop display. You can think of media queries as conditional statements, just as an "if" statement would only run a piece of code if the condition was true. A media query is the same, its far more limited, but as are many things in CSS.

I'm positive you will have used a website and noticed that it looks different on a computer compared to a mobile phone, or even a tablet. This is thanks to the use of breakpoints, which are very similar to conditional statements in other languages such as C++. When a certain condition is met, such as screen size range, or, change in form factor, different CSS is applied to provide a better-suited layout.

Relative units

Let's cover what relative and static units are. Relative units take into account the other content and more specifically the content's size, whereas static units do not and have an absolute value regardless of the amount of content.

If relative units are not used then static units would be used, which essentially lays the content using fixed units such as pixels. With this method, a box with a width of 400px on an 800px screen would take half the width. But, if the screen size changes to 300px, the box will now be partially off screen. Again, this would not provide the reader with that seamless experience, which we aim to provide.

The units simply display your content relative to everything else, or, more specifically, the screen size or viewport. This allows us, as creators, to display content consistently. Take the previous example, if we would like to display the box at half the screen width, on an 800px screen the box would be 400px wide, and on a 600px screen the box would be 300px wide. Using percentages we can set the width to 50%, which forces the box to always be half the width of its parent container, making its size relative to the rest of the page's content.

Maximum and minimum values

Scaling our content is greatly dependent on the screen size. But with screens such as ultrawide monitors, scaling the content may make it too big, or even too small, on mobile devices. Using maximum and minimum values, we are able to set upper and lower limits providing us with readable and clear results.

Nested objects

If we displayed every object individually, we would have to make them all adjust accordingly, but nesting allows us to wrap elements using containers. Nested objects are like a paragraph tag, as they contain text, and any changes made to the paragraph tag, such as its position or color, also affect its contents. Objects nested within each other are affected by any change made to their parent containers. An object can be anything from text and images, to HTML tags/elements. Take a look at the following example:

```
<div>
    <p>
        This is the best paragraph in the world.
    </p>

    <span>
        Some random text.
    </span>

    <img src="epic.png" />
</div>
```

In this example, there are four elements—a `div`, paragraph, span, and image tag. The paragraph, span, and image tags are nested within the `div` tag. If the `div` tag's maximum width and background color were changed, this would affect all its child objects/tags. But if we were to make a change to the paragraph tag, such as changing its text color, this would not affect any other sibling tags or its parent tag. It would only have an affect on its contents/objects.

So, for example, if a container is moved or scaled, the content within the container is also updated. This is where pixels come in use. You may not always want a container to be displayed 10% from the right as, on mobile devices, 10% equates to a lot of real estate potentially being wasted; you could specify 50px instead for example.

Mobile or desktop first

You can design a website from a small screen such as a phone and scale it up or go the other way round and design it with a large screen in mind. There is actually no right or wrong answer. Depending on the intended target audience and the website's purpose, this will become clear to you. Usually, considering both angles at the same time is the best route to go down. Most responsive frameworks on the market have been designed with a mobile-first philosophy, but that doesn't mean you cannot use it for a desktop-first design; it is on you as the designer to decide how content should be displayed.

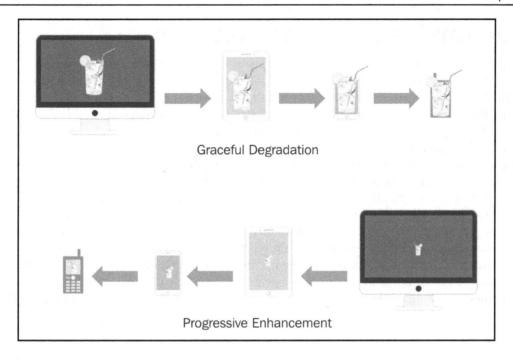

Graceful Degradation

Progressive Enhancement

Bitmaps versus vectors

Bitmaps are great for images with a lot of detail, such as backgrounds and usually logos. Common bitmap formats include .png and .jpg. But these images can be large in file size and require more bandwidth and time to load. On desktop devices this isn't too much of a problem, but on mobile devices that are heavily reliant on cellular services that don't always provide unlimited data, this can be problematic. Also, when scaling bitmaps, there is a loss in quality, which results in jagged and blurry images.

Vectors, on the other hand, are small in size and don't lose quality when scaling. I know you'll be tempted to scream, "Hail vectors!" at this book, but they do have their drawbacks. They are only useful for simple content such as icons. Also some older browsers do not fully support vectors.

Again there is no "right choice"; depending on the content to be displayed, bitmaps or vectors should be used.

Responsive grids and columns

The grid system is one of the universal concepts of Responsive Web Design, regardless of the framework a website is built upon. To put it simply, websites are split into rows and columns, and if an object/element occupies half the number of columns, it will always occupy that many regardless of the screen's size. So an element that occupies 3 of the 12 rows will occupy 25% of the width of its parent container, hence providing responsive design. This is great for small variations in screen sizes, but when a website is viewed on platforms varying from desktops to mobiles, then breakpoints are introduced as covered previously. Though there is no fixed number of columns that a responsive website should have, 12 is a common number used by some of the most popular and widespread frameworks. A framework in this context is anything built on top of the built-in web features. JavaScript is a web feature, but jQuery is a framework built on top of that to allow easier manipulation of the website using prewritten libraries/code. Though a framework isn't absolutely necessary, neither is using an off-the-shelf web browser. You could create your own, but it would be an immense waste of time, and the case for using a responsive framework is essentially the same. The following is an example of a basic responsive grid:

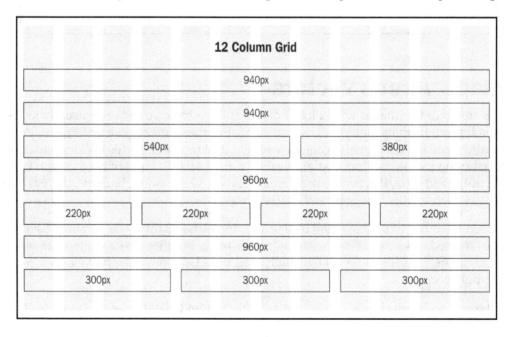

Rows allow us as developers to group content together, though there will be a fixed number of columns, not all columns have to be filled to go to the next row. A new row can be used explicitly, as can be seen in the following example:

Item 1

Lorem ipsum dolor sit amet, consectetur adipiscing elit.

Item 2

Lorem ipsum dolor sit amet, consectetur adipiscing elit.

Item 3

Lorem ipsum dolor sit amet, consectetur adipiscing elit, sed do eiusmod tempor incididunt ut labore et dolore magna aliqua. Ut enim ad minim veniam, quis nostrud exercitation ullamco laboris nisi ut aliquip ex ea commodo consequat.

Item 4

Lorem ipsum dolor sit amet, consectetur adipiscing elit.

Item 5

Lorem ipsum dolor sit amet, consectetur adipiscing elit, sed do eiusmod tempor incididunt ut labore et dolore magna aliqua. Ut enim ad minim veniam, quis nostrud exercitation ullamco laboris nisi ut aliquip ex ea commodo consequat.

Item 6

Lorem ipsum dolor sit amet, consectetur adipiscing elit.

Item 7

Lorem ipsum dolor sit amet, consectetur adipiscing elit, sed do eiusmod tempor incididunt ut labore et dolore magna aliqua. Ut enim ad minim veniam, quis nostrud exercitation ullamco laboris nisi ut aliquip ex ea commodo consequat.

Item 8

Lorem ipsum dolor sit amet, consectetur adipiscing elit.

This may be different to how you have developed websites in the past, but if there is anything you are unsure about don't worry, as things will become clearer when we start working on projects in future chapters.

Summary

In this chapter, we covered what responsive design is and the philosophies that make it so great and essential to the future of the web. The next chapter will cover what Bootstrap is and how it relates to Responsive Web Design.

2

What is Bootstrap, Why Do We Use It?

This chapter will explain what **Bootstrap** is, and how it relates to **Responsive Web Design** and its immense importance to the web industry.

The topics covered in this chapter are as follows:

- Bootstrap's history
- Bootstrap's syntax
- Bootstrap's grid system
- Bootstrap's responsive philosophy
- Bootstrap's components

Brief history of Bootstrap

In 2011, Bootstrap was created by two Twitter employees (Mark Otto and Jacob Thornton) to address the issue of fragmentation of internal tools/platforms. Bootstrap aimed to provide consistency among different web applications that were internally developed to reduce redundancy and increase adaptability and reusability. As digital creators, we should always aim to make our applications adaptable and reusable. This will help keep coherency between applications and speed up processes, as we won't need to create basic foundations over and over again. For example, a website might have a login system, which is not unique to one project, but prevalent in many, and therefore reusing already existing code for this makes sense.

After a few months, **Twitter Blueprint** was born and provided a way to document and share common design patterns/assets within Twitter. This alone is an amazing feature that would make Bootstrap an extremely useful framework to use. Then more internal developers began contributing towards the Bootstrap project as part of Hackathon week, and the project just exploded. Not long after, it was renamed "Bootstrap" as we know and love it today, and it was released as an open source project to the community. A core team led by Mark and Jacob along with a passionate and growing community of developers, helped to accelerate the growth of Bootstrap.

In early 2012 after a lot of contributions from the core team and the community, Bootstrap 2 was born. It had come a long way from being a framework for providing internal consistency among Twitter tools. It was now a responsive framework using a 12-column grid system. It also provided inbuilt support for *Glyphicons* and a plethora of other new components.

In 2013, Bootstrap 3 was released with a mobile-first approach to design and a fully redesigned set of components using the immensely popular flat design. This is the version many websites use today and it is very suitable for most developers. Bootstrap 4 is in active development with Alpha v6 being the latest stable release, as of writing this book.

Why use Bootstrap?

You probably have a reasonable idea of why you would use Bootstrap for developing websites after reading its history, but there is more to it. Simply put, it provides the following:

- A responsive grid, using the design philosophies mentioned in the first chapter.
- Cross browser compatibility, using `Normalize.css` to ensure elements render consistently across all browsers, (not a very easy task, I might add, speaking from experience). You might be wondering why it's difficult. Simply put, there are several different browsers, each with a plethora of versions, which all render content differently. I've seen some browsers put a border around an image by default, whereas some browsers don't. This type of inconsistency will prove to be very bad for user experience.

- A plethora of UI components, by providing polished UI components as developers, we are going to bring our creativity to life in a much easier way. These components usually allow a team to increase their development velocity, since they start from a solid tried and tested foundation. They not only provide good design, but they are usually implemented using best practices in terms of performance and accessibility.
- A very compact size with only a small footprint.
- Really fast to develop with, it doesn't get in the way like many other frameworks, but allows your creativity to shine through.
- Extremely easy to start using Bootstrap in your website.
- Bundles common JavaScript plugins such as **jQuery**.
- Excellent documentation.
- Customizable, allowing you to remove any unnecessary features.
- An amazing community that is always ready, 24/7, to help.

Why Bootstrap?

It's pretty clear now that Bootstrap is an amazing framework and that it will help provide consistency among our projects and aid cross browser responsive design. But why use Bootstrap over other frameworks? There are endless responsive frameworks like Bootstrap out there, such as Foundation, W3.CSS, and Skeleton, to mention a few.

Bootstrap, however, was one of the first responsive frameworks and is by far the most developed with an ever-growing community. It has documentation online, both official and unofficial, and other frameworks aren't able to boast about their resources as much as Bootstrap can. Constantly being updated, it makes it the right choice for any website developer.

Also, most JavaScript frameworks, such as Angular and React, have bindings to Bootstrap components that will reduce the amount of code and time spent binding it with another framework. It can also be used with tools such as SASS to customize the components provided further.

Bootstrap's grid system

This section will cover what a responsive grid system is and how it is implemented with Bootstrap.

First, let's cover what a grid system is in general, regardless of the framework you choose to develop your amazing website on top of. Without using a framework, CSS would be used to implement the grid. However, a framework like Bootstrap handles all of the CSS side and provides us with easy-to-use classes. A responsive grid system is composed of two main elements:

- **Columns**: These are the horizontal containers for storing content on a single row
- **Rows**: These are top level containers for storing columns

Your website will have at least one row, but it can have more. Each row can contain containers that span a set number of columns. For example, if the grid system had 100 columns, then a container that spans 50 would be half the width of the browser and/or parent element.

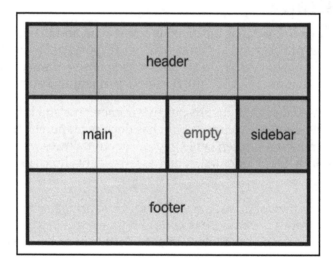

Basics

Bootstrap's grid system consists of 12 columns that can be used to display content. Bootstrap also uses containers (methods for storing the website's content), rows, and columns to aid in the layout and alignment of the web page's content. All of these employ HTML classes for usage and will be explained very shortly. The purpose of these are as follows:

- Columns are used to group snippets of the website's content, and they in turn allow manipulation without disrupting the internal content's flow. There are two different types of columns:
  - `.container`: Used for a fixed width, which is set by Bootstrap
  - `.container fluid`: Used for full width to span the entire browser

- Rows are used to horizontally group columns, which aids with lining up the site's content properly:
  - `.row`: There is only one type of row

- Columns mentioned previously are a way of setting how wide content should be. The following are the classes used for columns:
  - `.col-xs`: Designed to display the content only on extra-small screens
    - Max container width—none
    - Triggered when browser width is below 576px
  - `.col-sm`: Designed to display the content only on small screens
    - Max container width—540px
    - Triggered when browser width is above or equal to 576px and below 768px
  - `.col-md`: Designed to display the content only on medium screens
    - Max container width—720px
    - Triggered when browser width is above or equal to 768 and below 992px
  - `.col-lg`: Designed to display the content only on large screens
    - Max container width—960px
    - Triggered when browser width is above or equal to 992px and below 1200px

- `.col-xl`: Designed to display the content only on extra-large screens
  - Max container width—1140px
  - Triggered when browser width is above or equal to 1200px
- `.col`: Designed to be triggered on all screen sizes

To set a column's width, we simply append an integer ranging from 1 to 12 at the end of the class, like so:

- `.col-6`: Spans six columns on all screen sizes
- `.col-md-6`: Spans six columns only on extra-small screen sizes

Later in this chapter, we will run through some examples of how to use these features and how they work together.

Usage and examples

To use the aforementioned features, the structure is as follows:

- `div` with container class
  - `div` with row class
    - `div` with column class
      - Content
    - `div` with column class
      - Content
    - `div` with column class
      - Content
    - `div` with column class
      - Content
  - `div` with row class
    - `div` with column class
      - Content
    - `div` with column class
      - Content

- div with column class
  - Content
- div with column class
  - Content
- div with column class
  - Content
- div with column class
  - Content

The following examples may have some CSS styling applied; this does not affect their usage.

Equal width columns example

We will start off with a simple example that consists of one row and three equal columns on all screen sizes.

1 of 3	2 of 3	3 of 3

The following code produces the aforementioned result:

```
1  <div class="container">
2    <div class="row">
3      <div class="col">
4        1 of 3
5      </div>
6
7      <div class="col">
8        2 of 3
9      </div>
10
11     <div class="col">
12       3 of 3
13     </div>
14   </div>
15 </div>
```

You maybe scratching your head in regards to the column classes, as they have no numbers appended. This is an amazing feature that will come in useful very often. It allows us, as web developers, to add columns easily, without having to update the numbers, if the width, of the columns are equal. In this example, there are three columns, which means the three `divs` equally span their thirds of the row.

Multi-row, equal-width columns example

Now let's extend the previous example to multiple rows:

1 of 3	2 of 3	3 of 3
1 of 2		2 of 2

The following code produces the aforementioned result:

```
1  <div class="container">
2    <div class="row">
3      <div class="col">
4        1 of 3
5      </div>
6      <div class="col">
7        2 of 3
8      </div>
9      <div class="col">
10       3 of 3
11     </div>
12   </div>
13
14   <div class="row">
15     <div class="col">
16       1 of 2
17     </div>
18
19     <div class="col">
20       2 of 2
21     </div>
22   </div>
23 </div>
```

As you can see, by adding a new row, the columns automatically go to the next row. This is extremely useful for grouping content together.

Multi-row, equal-width columns without multiple rows example

The title of this example may seem confusing, but you need to read it correctly. We will now cover creating multiple rows using only a single row class. This can be achieved with the help of a display utility class called `w-100`.

1 of 3	2 of 3	3 of 3
1 of 2		2 of 2

The following code produces the aforementioned result:

```
1  <div class="container">
2    <div class="row">
3      <div class="col">1 of 3</div>
4      <div class="col">2 of 3</div>
5      <div class="col">3 of 3</div>
6
7      <div class="w-100"></div>
8
9      <div class="col">1 of 2</div>
10     <div class="col">2 of 2</div>
11   </div>
12 </div>
```

The example shows multiple row `div`s are not required for multiple rows. But the result isn't exactly identical, as there is no gap between the rows. This is useful for separating content that is still similar. For example, on a social network, it is common to have posts, and each post will contain information such as its date, title, description, and so on. Each post could be its own row, but within the post, the individual pieces of information could be separated using this class.

Differently sized columns

Up until now we have only created rows with equal-width columns. These are useful, but not as useful as being able to set individual sizes. As mentioned in the *Bootstrap grid system* section, we can easily change the column width by appending a number ranging from 1-12 at the end of the `col` class.

col-4	col-2	col-6

The following code produces the aforementioned result:

```
1  <div class="container">
2    <div class="row">
3      <div class="col-4">
4        col-4
5      </div>
6
7      <div class="col-2">
8        col-2
9      </div>
10
11     <div class="col-6">
12       col-6
13     </div>
14   </div>
15 </div>
```

As you can see, setting the explicit width of a column is very easy, but this applies the width to all screen sizes. You may want it only to be applied on certain screen sizes. The next section will cover this.

Differently sized columns with screen size restrictions

Let's use the previous example and expand it to change size responsively on differently sized screens. On extra-large screens, the grid will look like the following:

col-4	col-2	col-6

On all other screen sizes it will appear with equal-width columns:

col-4	col-2	col-6

The following code produces the aforementioned result:

```
1  <div class="container">
2    <div class="row">
3      <div class="col col-xl-4">
4        col-4
5      </div>
6
7      <div class="col col-xl-2">
8        col-2
9      </div>
10
11      <div class="col col-xl-6">
12        col-6
13      </div>
14    </div>
15  </div>
```

Now we are beginning to use breakpoints that provide a way of creating multiple layouts with minimal extra code to make use of the available real estate fully.

Mixing and matching

We aren't restricted to choosing only one break-point, we are able to set breakpoints for all the available screen sizes. The following figures illustrate all screen sizes, from extra-small to extra-large:

Extra-small:

Small:

1	2
3	4
5	6

Medium:

1	2	3
4	5	6

Large:

1	2	3	4
5	6		

Extra-large:

1	2	3	4	5	6

The following code produces the aforementioned results:

```
 1  <div class="container">
 2    <div class="row">
 3      <div class="col-xs-12 col-sm-6 col-md-4 col-lg-3 col-xl-2">
 4        1
 5      </div>
 6
 7      <div class="col-xs-12 col-sm-6 col-md-4 col-lg-3 col-xl-2">
 8        2
 9      </div>
10
11      <div class="col-xs-12 col-sm-6 col-md-4 col-lg-3 col-xl-2">
12        3
13      </div>
14
15      <div class="col-xs-12 col-sm-6 col-md-4 col-lg-3 col-xl-2">
16        4
17      </div>
18
19      <div class="col-xs-12 col-sm-6 col-md-4 col-lg-3 col-xl-2">
20        5
21      </div>
22
23      <div class="col-xs-12 col-sm-6 col-md-4 col-lg-3 col-xl-2">
24        6
25      </div>
26    </div>
27  </div>
```

It isn't necessary for all `div`s to have the same breakpoints or to have breakpoints at all.

Vertical alignment

The previous examples provide functionality for use cases, but sometimes the need may arise to align objects vertically. This could technically be done with empty `divs`, but this wouldn't be a very elegant solution. Instead there are alignment classes to help with this as can be seen here:

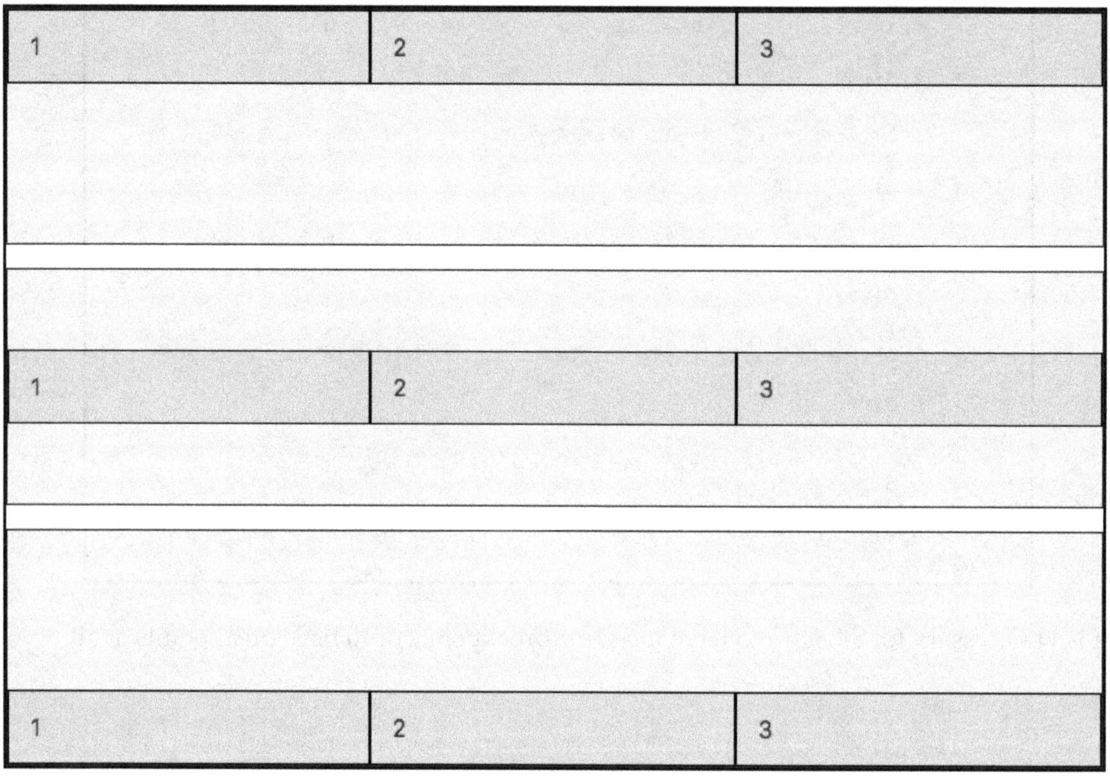

1	2	3
1	2	3
1	2	3

As we can see, you can align rows vertically in one of three positions. The following code produces the aforementioned result:

```
 1  <div class="container">
 2    <div class="row align-items-start">
 3      <div class="col">1</div>
 4      <div class="col">2</div>
 5      <div class="col">3</div>
 6    </div>
 7
 8    <div class="row align-items-center">
 9      <div class="col">1</div>
10      <div class="col">2</div>
11      <div class="col">3</div>
12    </div>
13
14    <div class="row align-items-end">
15      <div class="col">1</div>
16      <div class="col">2</div>
17      <div class="col">3</div>
18    </div>
19  </div>
```

We aren't restricted to only aligning rows, we can easily align columns relative to each other, as is demonstrated here:

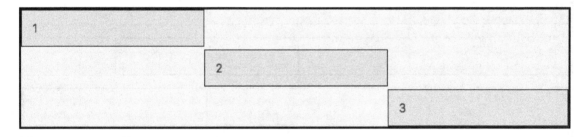

The following code produces the aforementioned result:

```
1  <div class="container">
2    <div class="row">
3      <div class="col align-self-start">
4        1
5      </div>
6
7      <div class="col align-self-center">
8        2
9      </div>
10
11     <div class="col align-self-end">
12       3
13     </div>
14   </div>
15 </div>
```

Horizontal alignment

As we vertically aligned content in the previous section, we will now cover how easy it is to align content horizontally. The following figures show the results of horizontal alignment:

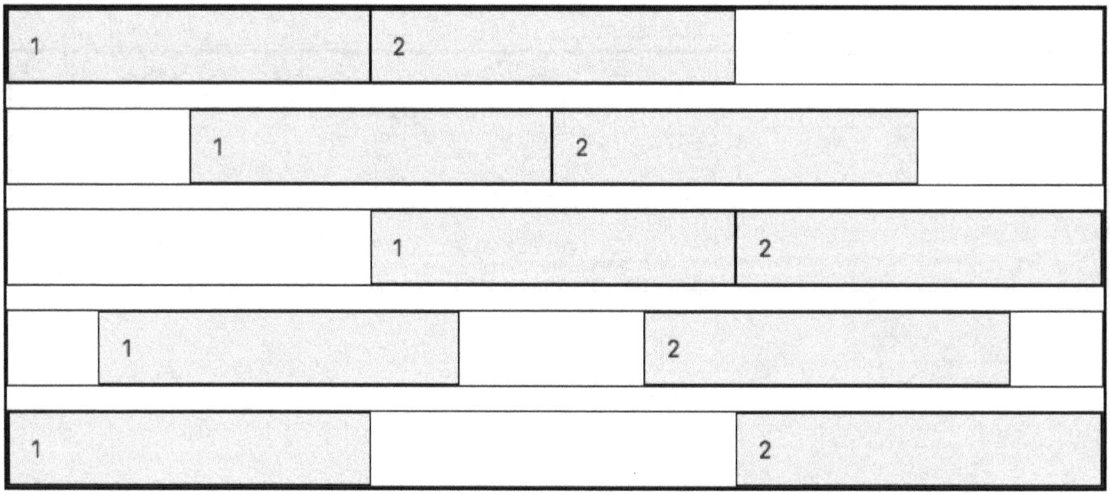

The following code produces the aforementioned result:

```
 1  <div class="container">
 2    <div class="row justify-content-start">
 3      <div class="col-4">1</div>
 4
 5      <div class="col-4">2</div>
 6    </div>
 7
 8    <div class="row justify-content-center">
 9      <div class="col-4">1</div>
10
11      <div class="col-4">2</div>
12    </div>
13
14    <div class="row justify-content-end">
15      <div class="col-4">1</div>
16
17      <div class="col-4">2</div>
18    </div>
19
20    <div class="row justify-content-around">
21      <div class="col-4">1</div>
22
23      <div class="col-4">2</div>
24    </div>
25
26    <div class="row justify-content-between">
27      <div class="col-4">1</div>
28
29      <div class="col-4">2</div>
30    </div>
31  </div>
```

Column offsetting

The need may arise to position content with a slight offset. If the content isn't centered or at the start or end, this can become problematic, but using column offsetting, we can overcome this issue. Simply add an offset class, with the screen size to target, and how many columns (1-12) the content should be offset by, as can be seen in the following example:

Column Size 2		Offset 2	
	Offset 3		

The following code produces the aforementioned result:

```
1  <div class="container">
2    <div class="row">
3      <div class="col-md-3">Column Size 2</div>
4      <div class="col-md-4 offset-md-2">Offset 2</div>
5    </div>
6    <div class="row">
7      <div class="col-md-3 offset-md-3">Offset 3</div>
8    </div>
9  </div>
```

Grid wrap up

The examples covered so far will suffice for most websites. There are more techniques for manipulating the grid, which can be found on Bootstrap's website `https://v4-alpha.getbootstrap.com/layout/grid/`

If you tried any of the examples, you may have noticed cascading from smaller screen-size classes to larger screen-size classes. This occurs when there are no explicit classes set for a certain screen size.

Bootstrap components

There is a plethora of amazing components that are provided with Bootstrap, thus saving time creating them from scratch. There are components for dropdowns, buttons, images, and so much more.

The usage is very similar to that of the grid system, and the same HTML elements we know and love are used with CSS classes to modify and display Bootstrap constructs. I won't go over every component that Bootstrap offers as that would require an encyclopedia in itself, and many of the commonly used ones will be covered in future chapters through example projects. I would however recommend taking a look at some of the components on Bootstrap's website `https://v4-alpha.getbootstrap.com/components/alerts/`

Summary

In this chapter, we covered what Bootstrap is and how its grid system will help us create our responsive websites. The next chapter will cover setting up a project template that can be reused for all our future projects.

3
Reusable Project Template

In this chapter, we will cover how to create a template for all future responsive websites, thus saving time and money. The topics covered in this chapter are as follows:

- Structured website template creation
- Header templating
- Footer templating
- Creating the main body of websites for all future projects
- Project structure overview

What is a reusable project template?

Most websites have a specific layout that is generic across most, if not all, of its pages. This is true for responsive and non-responsive websites. Usually, a website has a header and a footer that incorporate the website's brand and style and is used on all pages. Some websites also have a sidebar that is used on all pages.

Let's take a look at an example to illustrate this, let's look at YouTube. On the home page, a header and video recommendations appear:

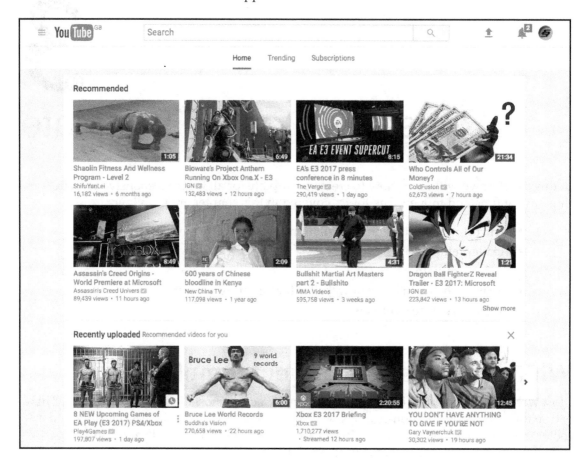

Scrolling to the bottom shows the footer with useful links after all of the video recommendations:

Now let's open a video and see how the top of the page looks:

As you can see, the header is identical and only the page's main content is different. Now let's look at the footer at the bottom of the page:

All of the preceding screenshots are from YouTube

The footer is also the same on both pages. I would recommend looking at more websites and seeing the similarities between the different pages.

If we were to create a website without a reusable project template, we would have to duplicate the header and footer code for every single page. Also, any changes such as a new logo in the header would require every single page to be updated, thus requiring more unnecessary time and creating an immense amount of redundancy. This can be very problematic when creating larger websites. I speak from experience, as many years ago, before I discovered the art of reusable project templates, I would literally add hundreds of lines of code on every single page and have to update all pages every single time a change was made.

Here is a list of some of the many benefits of using a reusable project structure:

- Save time rewriting code again and again and again
- Keep all code consistent and up to date
- Leads to leaner development times, always a bonus
- Can be reused outside of a single project, especially when other projects have similarities, thus immensely reducing the amount of time spent producing more projects, which will lead to increased productivity

Sounds amazing, let's talk about reusability in terms of a real-world scenario. Imagine that we are building a house. This encompasses a wide variety of tasks from mathematics, to engineering, all the way down to brick laying. Imagine if we had to reinvent all of that every single time, the house would never get built. Let's go even deeper. Take brick laying: we don't create the bricks, we buy them. The creator of the bricks doesn't reinvent the process behind constructing the bricks every single time, they reuse a template again and again and again. This immensely reduces the time and money required to produce a brick, which all leads to the house being built faster.

The concept of a reusable project template for websites is very similar to the preceding example. The code that is to be reused on many pages is abstracted into separate files, such as a header and a footer file, which follows the component-based methodology. This allows us to easily reuse components instead of rewriting them every single time. All that needs to be done on all the pages is to include the header and footer files. By including the abstracted components we immediately, with zero effort, have the design and functionality repeated. Any changes made to these files propagate throughout all the pages they are included in. The following is some pseudo code for this:

- Include `HEADER_FILE`
- Main content for page
- Include `FOOTER_FILE`

Development environment prerequisites

For normal frontend-only websites, we start by creating the code files and running them directly in a browser for testing. But this doesn't allow us to create a reusable project template, as we discussed previously. To create a template like this, we need a backend server-side language. I have chosen to use PHP, but any language will suffice, and this template will be easy to adapt. If you do have any queries regarding this, feel free to post them on my education platform, at `www.sonarlearning.co.uk`.

Even though this book is a frontend web development book, we will cover some server-side code, but it isn't crucial to responsive web design and will be very minimal. It will simply speed up the process of creating multiple pages and projects.

To use a backend language we will require a server, not necessarily a physical server that we have bought or a rented server from a hosting provider. We are able to set up a local server for free, which is fantastic. I will be using **XAMPP** (`https://www.apachefriends.org/index.html`) as it is cross-platform and works with macOS, Windows, and Linux. XAMPP supports PHP and Perl, however setting up a server for other languages is extremely simple with the appropriate tools. The following link can be used to set up a server: `http://www.sonarlearning.co.uk/coursepage.php?topic=course=php7newfeaturesvideoindex=12836#12836`

 For more information regarding setting up XAMPP take a look at the following website `http://www.tutorialspoint.com/articles/run-a-php-program-in-xampp-server`

Once you have set up your server, you are ready to create your reusable project template.

Creating our reusable project template

Now we will finally write some code; I hear everyone rejoicing! This section will cover the creation of our reusable project template and what forms the design decisions of its features.

Simple Bootstrap example

Let's create a basic Bootstrap project before we begin abstraction to turn it into a reusable project template. I would recommend creating a folder for your project on your server to store all your project's files. This will help you immensely when creating more projects, as everything will be separated and it will reduce the problem in the future of having too many files to manage.

Create a file called `index.html`, which will be the main entry point for our website, and put the following code inside of it. For this section, I would recommend copying the code from our GitHub page, as the CSS and JavaScript files are stored on a **Content Delivery Network** (**CDN**), which simply is an external server that feeds content to different sites and the links can be very long. The GitHub link is `https://github.com/PacktPublishing/Responsive-Web-Design-by-Example`

```
1  <!DOCTYPE html>
2  <html lang="en">
3    <head>
4      <!-- Required meta tags -->
5      <meta charset="utf-8">
6      <meta name="viewport" content="width=device-width,
       initial-scale=1, shrink-to-fit=no">
7
8      <!-- Bootstrap CSS -->
9      <link rel="stylesheet" href="https://maxcdn.bootstrapcdn.com/
       bootstrap/4.0.0-alpha.6/css/bootstrap.min.css" integrity="
       sha384-rwoIResjU2yc3z8GV/NPeZWAv56rSmLldC3R/
       AZzGRnGxQQKnKkoFVhFQhNUwEyJ" crossorigin="anonymous">
10   </head>
11   <body>
12     <h1>Hello, world!</h1>
13
14     <!-- jQuery first, then Tether, then Bootstrap JS. -->
15     <script src="https://code.jquery.com/jquery-3.1.1.slim.min.js"
       integrity="sha384-A7FZj7v+d/sdmMqp/nOQwliLvUsJfDHW+k9Omg/a/
       EheAdgtzNs3hpfag6Ed950n" crossorigin="anonymous"></script>
16     <script src="https://cdnjs.cloudflare.com/ajax/libs/tether/1.4.0/
       js/tether.min.js" integrity="sha384-DztdAPBWPRXSA/3eYEEUWrWCy7G5K
       Fbe8fFjk5JAIxUYHKkDx6Qin1DkWx51bBrb" crossorigin="anonymous"></
       script>
17     <script src="https://maxcdn.bootstrapcdn.com/
       bootstrap/4.0.0-alpha.6/js/bootstrap.min.js" integrity="sha384-vB
       WWzlZJ8ea9aCX4pEW3rVHjgjt7zpkNpZk+02D9phzyeVkE+jo0ieGizqPLForn"
       crossorigin="anonymous"></script>
18   </body>
19 </html>
```

Running the `index.html` file will produce the following result:

```
Hello, world!
```

Our website doesn't look very impressive, but it is now set up to use Bootstrap, which provides us with a plethora of features, from the grid to various CSS components that were discussed in the previous chapter.

Abstraction

Now we have a Bootstrap project set up, we can begin abstracting. If we don't, we would need to duplicate this code every single time a new page is to be created, and even more code will need to be duplicated once we have created a header and a footer, thus leading to immense redundancy. Let's check out the steps required for abstraction:

1. The first thing we need to do is rename `index.html` to `index.php`:

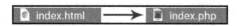

 At this point, we can no longer run the website by double-clicking the file, we need a server, which we have already set up.

2. Next, create a folder called `SNIPPETS`, with two PHP files inside of it called `HEADER.php` and `FOOTER.php`. Our project folder will look like the following screenshot:

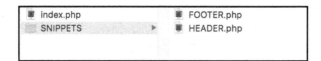

3. The `HEADER.php` file will contain all the code that includes style sheets, sets metadata, and other generic header code. Remove the following code from the `index.php` file and put it into the `HEADER.php` file:

```
1  <!DOCTYPE html>
2  <html lang="en">
3    <head>
4      <!-- Required meta tags -->
5      <meta charset="utf-8">
6      <meta name="viewport" content="width=device-width,
         initial-scale=1, shrink-to-fit=no">
7
8      <!-- Bootstrap CSS -->
9      <link rel="stylesheet" href="https://
         maxcdn.bootstrapcdn.com/bootstrap/4.0.0-alpha.6/css/
         bootstrap.min.css" integrity="sha384-rwoIResjU2yc3z8GV/
         NPeZWAv56rSmLldC3R/AZzGRnGxQQKnKkoFVhFQhNUwEyJ"
         crossorigin="anonymous">
10   </head>
11   <body>
```

4. Now, let's move onto the FOOTER.php. This will contain all the code at the bottom of the page, such as the visual footer and JavaScript include lines. Remove the following code from the index.php file and put it into the FOOTER.php file:

```
1    <!-- jQuery first, then Tether, then Bootstrap JS. -->
2    <script src="https://code.jquery.com/
     jquery-3.1.1.slim.min.js" integrity="sha384-A7FZj7v+d/
     sdmMqp/nOQwliLvUsJfDHW+k90mg/a/EheAdgtzNs3hpfag6Ed950n"
     crossorigin="anonymous"></script>
3    <script src="https://cdnjs.cloudflare.com/ajax/libs/
     tether/1.4.0/js/tether.min.js" integrity="sha384-DztdAP
     BWPRXSA/3eYEEUWrWCy7G5KFbe8fFjk5JAIxUYHKkDx6Qin1DkWx51b
     Brb" crossorigin="anonymous"></script>
4    <script src="https://maxcdn.bootstrapcdn.com/
     bootstrap/4.0.0-alpha.6/js/bootstrap.min.js" integrity=
     "sha384-vBWWzlZJ8ea9aCX4pEW3rVHjgjt7zpkNpZk+02D9phzyeVk
     E+jo0ieGizqPLForn" crossorigin="anonymous"></script>
5  </body>
6  </html>
```

5. Now the index.php file will contain the following code:

```
1
2    <h1>Hello, world!</h1>
3
4
```

6. And if run, it will produce the following:

```
Hello, world!
```

At first glance, the result looks identical to before, but if you were to try and use any Bootstrap code or code from any other libraries such as jQuery, it would not work. This is because that file no longer has the code it did before, but we can easily solve this by adding the `HEADER.php` and `FOOTER.php` files into our `index.php` code. Update the `index.php` file to look like the following:

```php
1  <?php require_once( "SNIPPETS/HEADER.php" ); ?>
2
3  <h1>Hello, world!</h1>
4
5  <?php require_once( "SNIPPETS/FOOTER.php" ); ?>
```

The `require_once` lines simply get the code from a particular file and insert it when this method is called. This allows us to create many files without duplicating the header and footer code. Also, any changes made to the header or footer files will propagate throughout our website as there is a single code base, thus immensely reducing redundancy.

The website will produce the same result visually, but it is set up for Bootstrap and any other library we include.

All of a page's main code should go between the two `require_once` lines, as can be seen in the preceding screenshot. We now have a reusable project template that we can use for all pages and projects, and easily extend when the need for more features arises.

Extending the header

We have abstracted the header code that sets up the headers for Bootstrap. This doesn't visually provide anything such as a navigation bar that most websites have universally across all of their pages.

This section will cover creating a navigation bar that consists of the following:

- Logo
- Buttons
- Collapsible navigation
- Search bar

Add the following code to the bottom of the `HEADER.php` file:

```
1  <nav class="navbar navbar-toggleable-md navbar-inverse
   bg-inverse">
2    <button class="navbar-toggler navbar-toggler-right" type=
     "button" data-toggle="collapse" data-target="
     #navbarTogglerDemo02" aria-controls="navbarTogglerDemo02"
      aria-expanded="false" aria-label="Toggle navigation">
3      <span class="navbar-toggler-icon"></span>
4    </button>
5
6    <a class="navbar-brand" href="index.php">
7      <img src="http://res.cloudinary.com/sonarsystems/image/
       upload/c_scale,w_150/v1442498022/
       Sonar-Systems-Circle-Logo_quet2k.png" width="30" height
       ="30" alt="">
8    </a>
9
10   <div class="collapse navbar-collapse" id="
     navbarTogglerDemo02">
11     <ul class="navbar-nav mr-auto mt-2 mt-md-0">
12       <li class="nav-item active">
13         <a class="nav-link" href="#">Home <span class="
           sr-only">(current)</span></a>
14       </li>
15       <li class="nav-item">
16         <a class="nav-link" href="#">Link</a>
17       </li>
18     </ul>
19
20     <form class="form-inline my-2 my-lg-0">
21       <input class="form-control mr-sm-2" type="text"
         placeholder="Search">
22
23       <button class="btn btn-outline-success my-2 my-sm-0"
         type="submit">Search</button>
24     </form>
25   </div>
26 </nav>
```

This will produce the following result:

On mobile devices, the following layout is displayed:

I will leave it to you to unveil the surprise that is the collapsible menu when the button on the right is pressed.

There is quite a lot of code, so let's go through it line by line:

- **Line 1** creates a navigation bar with some basic settings using CSS classes. The inverse classes refer to the navigation bar being dark; as an extra task try removing them. We also set at which breakpoint it should show a collapsed menu, that is, mobile. We have chosen medium, but it can easily be changed. Try setting it to extra small.
- **Lines 2-4** create the burger button that appears on smaller screens to open the collapsed navigation bar with some basic generic properties.
- **Lines 6-8** create the logo, which can easily be replaced with your own image be it stored locally or on a CDN. The image is enclosed in anchor tag to navigate back to the home page when clicked. This will become useful when we have multiple pages.
- **Lines 10-25** create the menu that appears within the navigation bar and also sets it to be collapsible. Using an unordered list, we created two regular text buttons that can be used to navigate to different parts of our website. Then, using a form, we created a search bar and a button for activating the search.

 This book is about frontend responsive web design, so this will not be functional but can be hooked up to a database using your chosen server-side language.

- Finally, **line 26** closes the navigation bar element.

As usual, I would recommend experimenting with the code and changing or removing classes to see how everything works and to understand it in more depth.

Extending the footer

As we did with the header, it's time to extend the footer to show visual elements that can be used for navigation and for providing useful information to the user across pages.

Add the following code to the top of the FOOTER.php file:

```
1  <footer class="footer">
2    <hr />
3
4    <div class="container">
5      <span>Awesome Footer 2017</span>
6    </div>
7  </footer>
```

This will produce the following result:

The footer has one problem, it's at the bottom, after the content. It should be situated/anchored at the bottom of the page, regardless of the amount of content on the page. To achieve this we need some CSS, so create a CSS folder inside your project's root directory and create an index.css file inside of it, like so:

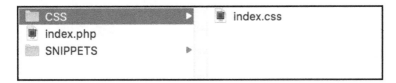

Put the following code inside the `index.css` file:

```
1  footer
2  {
3      position: absolute;
4      bottom: 0;
5      width: 100%;
6  }
```

This code will ensure our footer remains at the bottom and is 100% of the browser's width. Before this styling is applied we need to include the CSS file inside of our HEADER.php, like so:

```
1  <!DOCTYPE html>
2  <html lang="en">
3    <head>
4      <!-- Required meta tags -->
5      <meta charset="utf-8">
6      <meta name="viewport" content="width=device-width,
         initial-scale=1, shrink-to-fit=no">
7
8      <!-- Bootstrap CSS -->
9      <link rel="stylesheet" href="https://
         maxcdn.bootstrapcdn.com/bootstrap/4.0.0-alpha.6/css/
         bootstrap.min.css" integrity="sha384-rwoIResjU2yc3z8GV/
         NPeZWAv56rSmLldC3R/AZzGRnGxQQKnKkoFVhFQhNUwEyJ"
         crossorigin="anonymous">
10
11     <link rel="stylesheet" href="CSS/index.css" />
12   </head>
```

Now our website will look like this:

Extending the main body

At the moment we have some simple text inside of our `index.php` file, which serves as the body of the page. The code doesn't conform to Bootstrap guidelines of using containers and rows, which we covered in the previous section. Update the `index.php` file with the following code:

```php
1  <?php require_once( "SNIPPETS/HEADER.php" ); ?>
2
3  <div class="container">
4    <div class="row">
5      <h1>Hello, world!</h1>
6    </div>
7  </div>
8
9  <?php require_once( "SNIPPETS/FOOTER.php" ); ?>
```

This code produces the following result:

It may look like the only thing that has changed is that the text is now indented. However, behind the scenes we are taking advantage of Bootstrap's grid system, and this allows us to use responsive columns.

 Bootstrap recommends not to nest containers and only have a single container on a page unless you need regular and fluid containers.

Troubleshooting

We have covered a lot of content, here are some common pitfalls you may encounter.

PHP errors

If you come across any PHP errors at this stage, they will most likely be referring to the `require` lines. Just make sure the directory and the file you are trying to use exist and are named correctly. Any errors referring to this will look like this:

> **Warning**: require_once(SNIPPETS/HEADE.php): failed to open stream: No such file or directory in **/Applications/XAMPP/xamppfiles/htdocs/RWD/index.php** on line **1**
>
> **Fatal error**: require_once(): Failed opening required 'SNIPPETS/HEADE.php' (include_path='.:/Applications/XAMPP/xamppfiles/lib/php') in **/Applications/XAMPP/xamppfiles/htdocs/RWD/index.php** on line **1**

CSS not applying

If no CSS is being applied, this is most likely due to the code incorrectly referring to the file. This can happen for the following reasons:

- Incorrect file/directory name
- Incorrect file/directory location
- File/directory not created

Summary

In this chapter, we have covered how to set up Bootstrap and abstract common functionality to create a reusable project template for all of our projects. The next chapter will cover starting our first project: creating a single-page portfolio website.

4
Creating the Introduction Section

In this chapter, we will create the first section of our single-page portfolio website, which will be an introduction section. This section will act as the first point of call for the user as they load up the website.

The topics covered in this chapter are as follows:

- Anchoring this section to the overall single-page website design flow
- Responsive full-width image
- Bootstrap jumbotron
- Bootstrap/HTML headers
- Bootstrap/HTML subheaders
- Debugging and testing responsive design

What is a single-page website?

You may be wondering what a single-page website is and whether you have ever used one. Simply put, it's a website with only a single page split into sections, using buttons to anchor to the different sections. These sections usually contain little information; they are essentially the equivalent of separate pages in a larger website.

Single-page websites are commonly used for the following types of websites:

- Portfolio
- Landing page

- Coming soon page
- App page
- Simple gallery
- Product page

Single-page examples

Let's take a look at some awesome single-page examples.

Android KitKat promotional homepage

When scrolling, elements animate and scroll across the screen. There is a set of navigation buttons in the form of circles on the right-hand side. Clicking one of these makes the website scroll to that section; it doesn't jump, but scrolls to it, which provides a more seamless experience for the user. This isn't necessary, but it improves the UX.

Here's the website link: https://www.kitkat.com/android/#/home

GoldSquare

This is a simpler example with little animation. When a button is pressed on the navigation bar, the page simply scrolls to the desired section. This is simple yet effective:

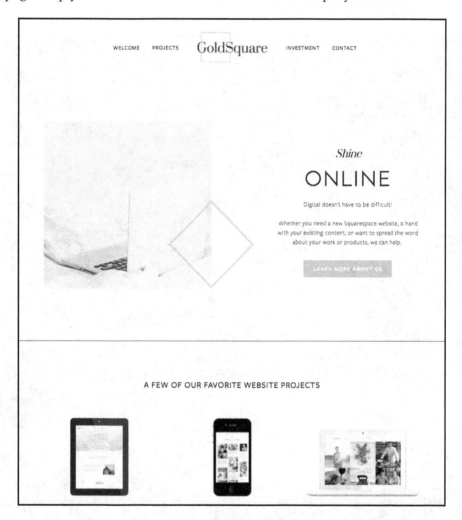

The website link is: `http://www.goldsquare.co`

Anthony Designer

This website takes a very unique approach to navigation, with a heavy use of animations. Instead of scrolling vertically, the site uses cards and scrolls horizontally, but with a system of navigation, using horizontal buttons:

The website link is: http://www.anthonydesigner.com/

Richman

This website provides some simple animation along with anchoring, thus presenting a wonderful and elegant website:

The website link for this is: http://richman-kcm.com/

Implementing our introduction section

We will now create an introduction section for our single-page portfolio website. This can be easily modified with the content that your site needs.

The introduction section, as the name suggests, is used to introduce the viewer to the rest of the website. With the use of images and text, the viewer will be able to understand the subject matter of the website.

What is a jumbotron?

A **jumbotron** may sound like a robot from an upcoming Transformers movie, but it is a really cool feature of Bootstrap. Bootstrap borrowed the term from the big displays that are used at sporting events, as it provides a means for prominently displaying information:

http://assets.sbnation.com/assets/2481507/rizzosign.jpg

A jumbotron in Bootstrap is actually a very simple concept; it is essentially a HTML element used to contain text and images in a large, poster-like fashion.

Unfortunately, our site won't have one of them, but you can add the image into the jumbotron.

Implementing a basic jumbotron

Let's start off by adding a simple jumbotron so that we can see how it works. Add the following code to the `index.php` file so that it looks like the following:

```
1  <?php require_once( "SNIPPETS/HEADER.php" ); ?>
2
3  <div class="jumbotron jumbotron-fluid">
4    <div class="container">
5      <h1 class="display-3">Fluid jumbotron</h1>
6      <p class="lead">This is a modified jumbotron that
         occupies the entire horizontal space of its parent.</p>
7    </div>
8  </div>
9
10 <?php require_once( "SNIPPETS/FOOTER.php" ); ?>
```

You have most likely noticed that the pre-existing code has been removed. This is due to it not being required at the moment; it will be different for each project and was used as a placeholder.

Whenever I refer to code in a `.php` file, I mean the code between the `require` lines, also known as the non-PHP code. So, if I were to tell you to put the following code at the end of the `index.php` file code:

```
1  <div>Awesome Div</div>
```

I don't mean add the code like this:

```php
1  <?php require_once( "SNIPPETS/HEADER.php" ); ?>
2
3  <div class="jumbotron jumbotron-fluid">
4    <div class="container">
5      <h1 class="display-3">Fluid jumbotron</h1>
6      <p class="lead">This is a modified jumbotron that
       occupies the entire horizontal space of its parent.</p>
7    </div>
8  </div>
9
10 <?php require_once( "SNIPPETS/FOOTER.php" ); ?>
11
12 <div>Awesome Div</div>
```

Instead, what I mean is this:

```php
1  <?php require_once( "SNIPPETS/HEADER.php" ); ?>
2
3  <div class="jumbotron jumbotron-fluid">
4    <div class="container">
5      <h1 class="display-3">Fluid jumbotron</h1>
6      <p class="lead">This is a modified jumbotron that
       occupies the entire horizontal space of its parent.</p>
7    </div>
8  </div>
9
10 <div>Awesome Div</div>
11
12 <?php require_once( "SNIPPETS/FOOTER.php" ); ?>
```

If I ever intend for you to modify or factor in the PHP code, which will only be the `require` lines in this book, then I will explicitly state it. Now that's out of the way, let's continue. The jumbotron code will produce the following result:

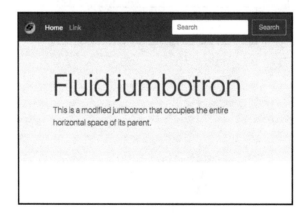

We now have a jumbotron; try resizing it and seeing how it reacts. Let's go through the code line by line:

- **Line 3** creates a div set up to be a jumbotron. The jumbotron-fluid class isn't required, but it forces the width of the jumbotron to match its parent width, which happens to be the body. Removing this class won't have any effect on our current website, but if you were to add a max-width on the body using CSS, then you would see the difference; as an extra task, I would recommend doing this.
- **Line 4** creates the container we know and love.
- **Line 5** creates a header using a Bootstrap-styled class.
- **Line 6** creates a paragraph using a Bootstrap-styled class.
- **Lines 7** and **8** close the jumbotron and container elements respectively.

 You can pretty much include anything inside the jumbotron, such as rows and images.

We have a working jumbotron, but it is a far cry from what we have seen on other single-page websites. This can be solved using images, CSS, and other elements. Let's do some of this now.

Adding an image to the jumbotron

We can add a simple image that appears with the rest of the content; we will add a background image as this is a very common standard. However, we will first cover changing the color of the background; let's change it to red. Add the following ID to the jumbotron:

```
3  <div class="jumbotron jumbotron-fluid" id="JumbotronID">
4    <div class="container">
5      <h1 class="display-3">Fluid jumbotron</h1>
6      <p class="lead">This is a modified jumbotron that
       occupies the entire horizontal space of its parent.</p>
7    </div>
8  </div>
```

Now, add the following CSS to the `index.css` file:

```
 1  footer
 2  {
 3      position: absolute;
 4      bottom: 0;
 5      width: 100%;
 6  }
 7
 8  #JumbotronID
 9  {
10      background: #e74c3c;
11      color: white;
12  }
```

I chose to change the text color to white as it is more visually striking on the red background. I have also chosen a different shade of red that conforms to modern flat design standards. Here's the result of our code:

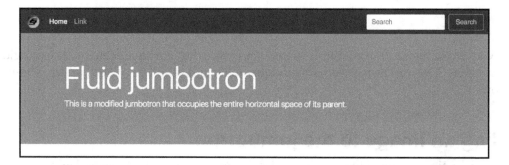

As you can see, even something as simple as changing the color can have a profound effect on how the content looks.

Let's add a background image; any image will suffice. Replace the container element in the `index.php` file with an image element that has an ID of `JumbotronImage`, as can be seen here:

```
1  <?php require_once( "SNIPPETS/HEADER.php" ); ?>
2
3  <div class="jumbotron jumbotron-fluid" id="JumbotronID">
4      <img id="JumbotronImage" src="https://res.cloudinary.com/
       sonarsystems/image/upload/v1497973720/
       Youtube_2Bnew_2Bheader_u0ruil.png" />
5  </div>
6
7  <?php require_once( "SNIPPETS/FOOTER.php" ); ?>
```

The preceding code produces the following result:

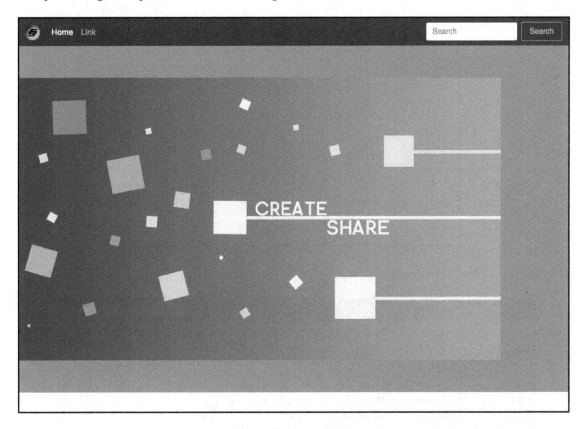

As you can see, this is less than ideal for the following reasons:

- The image doesn't occupy the width of the browser
- The image isn't responsive when the browser is resized
- There is padding in the jumbotron, which is visible as red empty space

First, let's fix the issue of the image not occupying the full width of the browser and not being responsive. This can be achieved by adding some simple CSS to constrain the image's width, as demonstrated:

```
 1  footer
 2  {
 3      position: absolute;
 4      bottom: 0;
 5      width: 100%;
 6  }
 7
 8  #JumbotronID
 9  {
10      background: #e74c3c;
11      color: white;
12  }
13
14  #JumbotronImage
15  {
16      width: 100%;
17  }
```

This produces the following result:

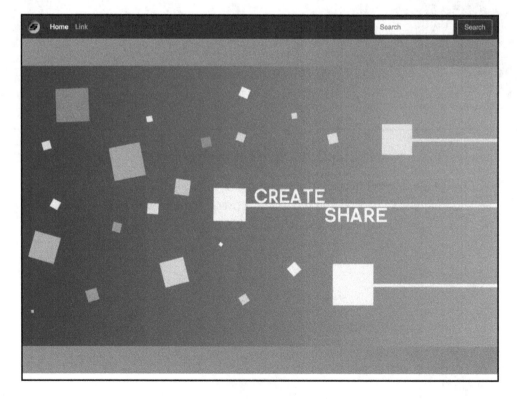

We are almost there; now we have to remove the red empty space. Removing the styling code from the jumbotron will not fix this, as it will just show the default grey color instead. We need to remove the padding, which can be done in CSS, as follows:

```
 8  #JumbotronID
 9  {
10      background: #e74c3c;
11      color: white;
12      padding: 0;
13  }
```

The preceding code produces the following result:

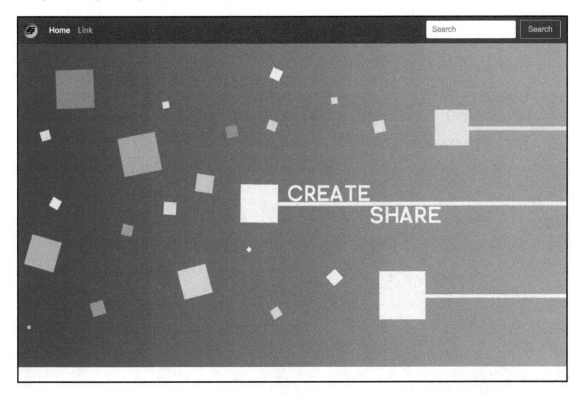

We now have a fully responsive image with no padding, which looks awesome. Many websites put text onto the image as well, not embedded in the image, but as a HTML element over the top. We will cover implementing this in the next section.

Combining text and images in a jumbotron

To add some text, we will use the same header tag and class we used before; it will be placed above the image, as follows:

```php
1  <?php require_once( "SNIPPETS/HEADER.php" ); ?>
2
3  <div class="jumbotron jumbotron-fluid" id="JumbotronID">
4    <h1 class="display-3">Heading</h1>
5
6    <img id="JumbotronImage" src="https://res.cloudinary.com/
     sonarsystems/image/upload/v1497973720/
     Youtube_2Bnew_2Bheader_u0ruil.png" />
7  </div>
8
9  <?php require_once( "SNIPPETS/FOOTER.php" ); ?>
```

The preceding code produces the following result:

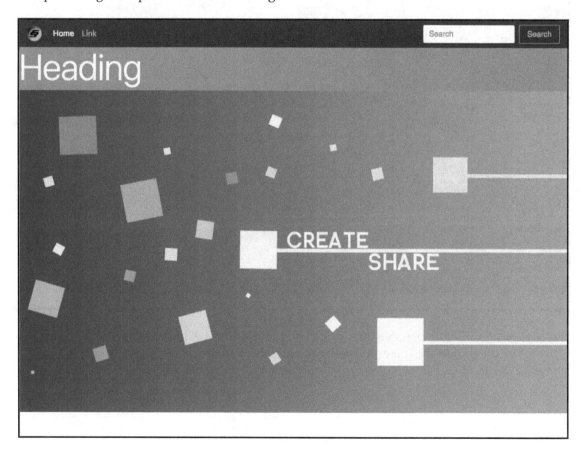

Though the heading has appeared, it is above the image, which is not what we wanted at all. We can ignore the background color behind the heading, as it can be anything, because it won't be shown once the text is on top of the image.

We need to change the positioning method used for the heading to `absolute`, which won't be positioned relatively to other objects. First, add a class of `jumbotronTextOnImages` to the heading, as shown:

```php
1  <?php require_once( "SNIPPETS/HEADER.php" ); ?>
2
3  <div class="jumbotron jumbotron-fluid" id="JumbotronID">
4    <h1 class="display-3 jumbotronTextOnImages">Heading</h1>
5
6    <img id="JumbotronImage" src="https://res.cloudinary.com/
     sonarsystems/image/upload/v1497973720/
     Youtube_2Bnew_2Bheader_u0ruil.png" />
7  </div>
8
9  <?php require_once( "SNIPPETS/FOOTER.php" ); ?>
```

Add the following CSS code to the `index.css` file:

```css
20  .jumbotronTextOnImages
21  {
22      position: absolute;
23  }
```

This will produce the following result:

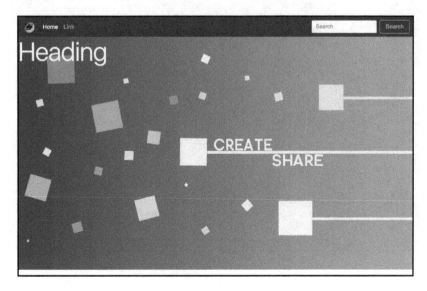

We are now getting somewhere. This still isn't very appealing; it will help if we center the text horizontally. This can be achieved by adding a built-in Bootstrap class called `text-center` to the heading, as illustrated:

```
1  <?php require_once( "SNIPPETS/HEADER.php" ); ?>
2
3  <div class="jumbotron jumbotron-fluid" id="JumbotronID">
4      <h1 class="display-3 jumbotronTextOnImages text-center">
        Heading</h1>
5
6      <img id="JumbotronImage" src="https://res.cloudinary.com/
        sonarsystems/image/upload/v1497973720/
        Youtube_2Bnew_2Bheader_u0ruil.png" />
7  </div>
8
9  <?php require_once( "SNIPPETS/FOOTER.php" ); ?>
```

This has no visual effect at the moment, because our heading has a position of absolute, which can mess with certain items. However, overcoming this issue is simple, simply add a `width` of `100%` to the `jumbotronTextOnImages` class:

```
20  .jumbotronTextOnImages
21  {
22      position: absolute;
23      width: 100%;
24  }
```

This will produce the following result:

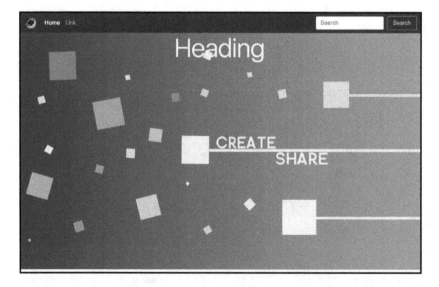

Many times, text isn't completely centered vertically, and is usually slightly off-center or a quarter of the way along, for example. We will do something similar with our heading; we will post it a little above the center. First, add an ID of `JumbotronHeading` to the heading:

```
1  <?php require_once( "SNIPPETS/HEADER.php" ); ?>
2
3  <div class="jumbotron jumbotron-fluid" id="JumbotronID">
4      <h1 class="display-3 jumbotronTextOnImages text-center"
        id="JumbotronHeading">Heading</h1>
5
6      <img id="JumbotronImage" src="https://res.cloudinary.com/
        sonarsystems/image/upload/v1497973720/
        Youtube_2Bnew_2Bheader_u0ruil.png" />
7  </div>
8
9  <?php require_once( "SNIPPETS/FOOTER.php" ); ?>
```

Add the following code to the `index.css` file for moving the text down:

```
26  #JumbotronHeading
27  {
28      margin-top: 20%;
29  }
```

This will now produce the following result:

Fantastic, but you may be wondering why we used an ID instead of adding the style code to move the heading down to the `jumbotronTextOnImages` class. The class is designed to be reusable with other elements that your site may have, but the positioning is more specific to this heading, hence the use of an ID over the pre-existing class.

You may think that the text will be better in a different color, and I would totally agree with you. As an extra task, change the color to something more suitable in relation to the background image, and also experiment with the positioning.

Anchoring a section to the navigation bar

If we go back to one of our single-page examples from earlier in this chapter (or any single-page website), you will notice that the navigation bar provides a means of actually navigating the website. Even though there is only a single page, there is often a tendency for the page to get pretty long. This isn't a problem, but one of the many great features of single-page websites; it still requires navigation using the conventional means of buttons. Let's go back to the *Richman* website and take a look. If we click on the **ABOUT** button, for example, it scrolls us down to the about section, as follows:

Let's implement this for our website. Update the `href` attribute of the `Home` button in the `HEADER.php` file to have the ID of `HomeSection`, as shown:

```
23      <div class="collapse navbar-collapse" id="
        navbarTogglerDemo02">
24        <ul class="navbar-nav mr-auto mt-2 mt-md-0">
25          <li class="nav-item active">
26            <a class="nav-link" href="#HomeSection">Home <
              span class="sr-only">(current)</span></a>
27          </li>
28          <li class="nav-item">
29            <a class="nav-link" href="#">Link</a>
30          </li>
31        </ul>
```

If you try clicking, nothing will happen at the moment because it hasn't been linked to the first section. Implementing the linkage is extremely simple, just add an ID of `HomeSection` to the jumbotron `div`, as demonstrated:

```
1  <?php require_once( "SNIPPETS/HEADER.php" ); ?>
2
3  <div class="jumbotron jumbotron-fluid" id="HomeSection">
4    <h1 class="display-3 jumbotronTextOnImages text-center"
       id="JumbotronHeading">Heading</h1>
5
6    <img id="JumbotronImage" src="https://res.cloudinary.com/
       sonarsystems/image/upload/v1497973720/
       Youtube_2Bnew_2Bheader_u0ruil.png" />
7  </div>
8
9  <?php require_once( "SNIPPETS/FOOTER.php" ); ?>
```

Before we even run our website, you may be scratching your head and thinking that there was an ID already assigned to the jumbotron `div`. You would be right; I have renamed it from `JumbotronID` to `HomeSection` as it accurately represents what the section is; there can be multiple jumbotrons. When you run the website, certain aspects such as styling will not be applied correctly; you need to go to the `index.css` file and update all instances of `HomeSection` and anywhere else you may be referring to it. At the moment, there is only one instance, which is in the `index.css` file.

You might be wondering why I didn't name it like that from the beginning. The main reason is, while programming anything you will have to go back and change things, especially the naming of objects and variables. Each change will come with its own bugs that need to be addressed, so getting into the swing of things now will help you better understand how to overcome those bugs.

If you run the website now, it will appear to do nothing when the **Home** button is clicked. However, if you look at the URL, there will be an anchored URL that will look similar to the following image with some slight variation depending on your website/server location:

It is clearly anchoring the home section; it is actually working, there just isn't enough content for it to actually move. You can confirm this by either resizing the browser's height to something very small or adding random content before the jumbotron `div`, and the anchoring will work.

We can leave the scrolling as is so that it works just fine. However, it doesn't actually scroll, but it snaps to the home section; it isn't a nice smooth scroll. The next section will cover animation for our scroll, or lack of scroll.

Animating our navigation bar anchor

Now it's time to implement some JavaScript. First, let's create a folder called `JS` at the root of our project directory, as follows:

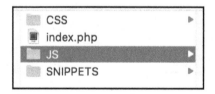

Now, create a JavaScript file called `index.js` inside the `JS` folder. After creation, the structure of your project will look like the following image:

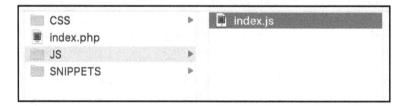

Now, let's include the `index.js` file into our `FOOTER.php` file using the following line:

```
1    <footer class="footer">
2      <hr />
3
4      <div class="container">
5        <span>Awesome Footer 2017</span>
6      </div>
7    </footer>
8
9    <!-- jQuery first, then Tether, then Bootstrap JS. -->
10   <script src="https://code.jquery.com/
     jquery-3.1.1.slim.min.js" integrity="sha384-   7FZj7v+d/
     sdmMqp/nOQwliLvUsJfDHW+k90mg/a/EheAdgtzNs3   fag6Ed950n"
      crossorigin="anonymous"></script>
11   <script src="https://cdnjs.cloudflare.com ajax/libs/
     tether/1.4.0/js/tether.min.js" integrity   sha384-DztdAP
     BWPRXSA/3eYEEUWrWCy7G5KFbe8fFjk5JAIxUYH  Dx6Qin1DkWx51b
     Brb" crossorigin="anonymous"></script>
12   <script src="https://maxcdn.bootstr  p  n.com/
     bootstrap/4.0.0-alpha.6/js/bootstra       js" integrity=
     "sha384-vBWWzlZJ8ea9aCX4pEW3rVHjgjt       NpZk+02D9phzyeVk
     E+jo0ieGizqPLForn" crossorigin="ano  ous"></script>
13
14   <script src="JS/index.js"></script>
15   </body>
16 </html>
```

 The file is included after the other scripts because it will use code from jQuery, and as your project expands it will most likely use features from the other files as well. You can also include JavaScript files in the header, but this means the website takes longer to load before anything is displayed. Users most likely wait for the website to load or for the majority of it to load before interacting with it, so having it visually appear as fast as possible is very important for all websites.

As you may expect, this produces nothing visually; we need to add the animation code inside the `index.js` file. However, before we do that, let's add an ID to the `NavBarHomeButton` button, which will allow us to easily detect the button in JavaScript. The `HEADER.php` file will feature the following change:

```
23   <div class="collapse navbar-collapse" id="
     navbarTogglerDemo02">
24     <ul class="navbar-nav mr-auto mt-2 mt-md-0">
25       <li class="nav-item active">
26         <a class="nav-link" id="NavBarHomeButton" href=
         "#HomeSection">Home <span class="sr-only">(
         current)</span>
27       </li>
28       <li class="nav-item">
29         <a class="nav-link" href="#">Link</a>
30       </li>
31     </ul>
```

Now, add the following code to the `index.js` file to smoothly scroll to the anchored section instead of snapping to its location:

```
 1  $( function( )
 2  {
 3      $( document ).on( 'click', '#NavBarHomeButton',
            function( event )
 4      {
 5          $( 'html, body' ).animate(
 6          {
 7              scrollTop: $("#HomeSection").offset().top
 8          }, 2000 );
 9
10
11          event.preventDefault();
12      } );
13  } );
```

Let's go through each line of code and its purpose:

- **Line 1** ensures that the JavaScript code is only triggered once the page has fully loaded, ensuring that the element is set up correctly before using it.
- **Line 3** checks whether the **Home** button in the navigation bar has been pressed by using a jQuery listener to detect clicks.
- **Line 5** is used to scroll within the website.
- **Line 7** sets which element to scroll to by getting its position from the top. The `scrollTop` functionality essentially scrolls to a particular point, hence the need for the top of the element's position.
- **Line 8** is used to specify the animation duration in milliseconds, which is set to 2000, that is, two seconds.
- **Line 11** prevents the default functionality of the click, which would have been the previous non-animated scroll.

If you go to the website and click on the **Home** button, it will not work. There will be an error in your browser's console related to the JavaScript code, which will look something like this:

```
⊗ ▶ Uncaught TypeError: $(...).animate is not a function
       at HTMLAnchorElement.<anonymous> (index.js:7)
       at HTMLDocument.dispatch (jquery-3.1.1.slim.min.js:3)
       at HTMLDocument.q.handle (jquery-3.1.1.slim.min.js:3)
  >
```

The exact error may vary depending on the browser you are testing the website with, but it will be something similar. The following website shows how to open the console on all browsers: `https://www.wickedlysmart.com/hfjsconsole/`

The reason for this error occurring is due to the jQuery version used with the Bootstrap template. It is the slim version that removes a lot of extra jQuery functionalities, including animation. To access animation, we need the full version; replace the jQuery `include` line in the footer with the following link: `https://code.jquery.com/jquery-3.2.1.min.js`

The `FOOTER.php` file will now look like this:

```
1    <footer class="footer">
2      <hr />
3
4      <div class="container">
5        <span>Awesome Footer 2017</span>
6      </div>
7    </footer>
8
9    <!-- jQuery first, then Tether, then Bootstrap JS. -->
10   <script src="https://code.jquery.com/
     jquery-3.2.1.min.js" integrity="
     sha256-hwg4gsxgFZhOsEEamdOYGBf13FyQuiTwlAQgxVSNgt4="
     crossorigin="anonymous"></script>
11   <script src="https://cdnjs.cloudflare.com/ajax/libs/
     tether/1.4.0/js/tether.min.js" integrity="sha384-DztdAP
     BWPRXSA/3eYEEUWrWCy7G5KFbe8fFjk5JAIxUYHKkDx6Qin1DkWx51b
     Brb" crossorigin="anonymous"></script>
12   <script src="https://maxcdn.bootstrapcdn.com/
     bootstrap/4.0.0-alpha.6/js/bootstrap.min.js" integrity=
     "sha384-vBWWzlZJ8ea9aCX4pEW3rVHjgjt7zpkNpZk+02D9phzyeVk
     E+jo0ieGizqPLForn" crossorigin="anonymous"></script>
13
14   <script src="JS/index.js"></script>
15   </body>
16 </html>
```

If you run the code, the website will now scroll to the **Home** section smoothly instead of snapping to it, assuming that you have content before that section, as mentioned earlier. Great! We have a scrolling single-page website, but we will have to duplicate the JavaScript code for every navigation button. This will lead to immense redundancy, which is what we are trying to avoid with the reusable project template. Instead, we will dynamically select the section from the button clicked on to navigate to. First, remove the ID on the `Home` button in the navigation bar and add a class called `navButton`; the navigation bar will now look like this:

```
23        <div class="collapse navbar-collapse" id="
          navbarTogglerDemo02">
24          <ul class="navbar-nav mr-auto mt-2 mt-md-0">
25            <li class="nav-item active">
26              <a class="nav-link navButton" href="
                #HomeSection">Home <span class="sr-only">(
                current)</span></a>
27            </li>
28            <li class="nav-item">
29              <a class="nav-link" href="#">Link</a>
30            </li>
31          </ul>
```

Now update the `index.js` file to look like the following code:

```
1  $( function( )
2  {
3      $( document ).on( 'click', '.navButton', function(
            event )
4      {
5          $( 'html, body' ).animate(
6          {
7              scrollTop: $( $( this ).attr('href') ).offset(
                  ).top
8          }, 2000 );
9
10
11          event.preventDefault( );
12      } );
13 } );
```

The following lines have been changed:

- **Line 3** checks whether a button with the class of `navButton` has been clicked.
- **Line 7** gets the `href` of the element the user has clicked on. This means that even if we decide to change the element to which a navigation button points, the JavaScript code will automatically have access to the new location, thus reducing redundancy.

The next section will cover fixing a problem you may have noticed with the footer.

Fixing footer visibility and the location problem

Our footer has a problem in that, when we scroll on small screens, the footer stays where it is, it doesn't remain at the bottom, as shown:

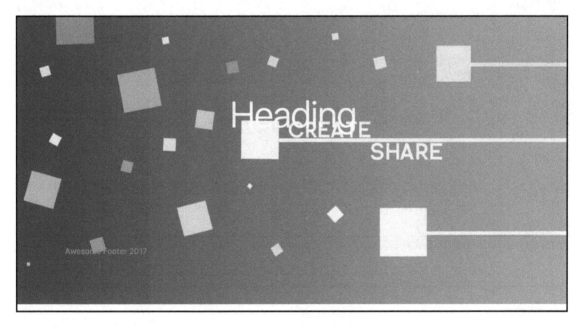

 I have made the footer text color red to illustrate the problem more clearly.

Fixing this is extremely simple; it actually requires us to remove code instead of adding any. Then, you may be wondering why I put the code in; this was intended to showcase some of the problems you may face. Just remove all style code related to the footer, which should be as follows:

```
1  footer
2  {
3      position: absolute;
4      bottom: 0;
5      width: 100%;
6  }
```

The website footer now will react like this:

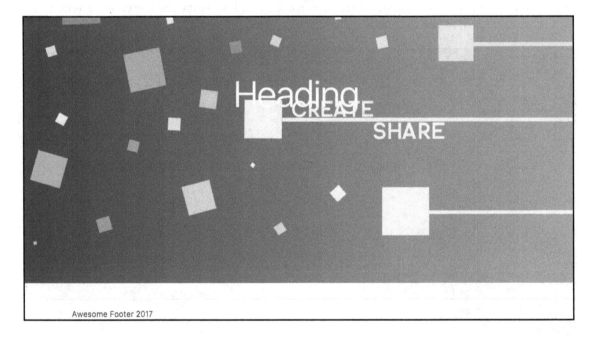

Awesome Footer 2017

Placing the header on top

Most single-page websites always place their headers (navigation bar) on top. This allows easy access to navigation even on long pages, leading to a more seamless experience. The Richman website example does this; I would recommend taking a look and seeing how it feels as a user. Just a quick reminder; here's a screenshot of the problem on our website that we are trying to fix:

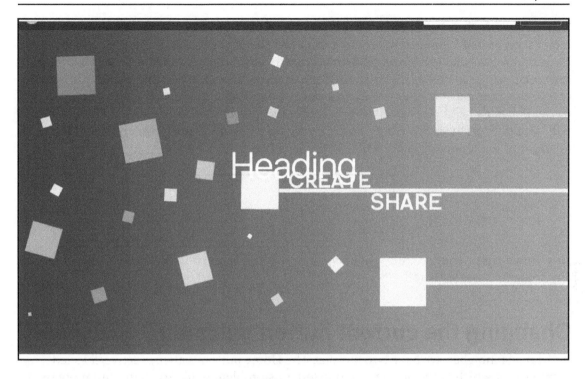

We want the content of the website to scroll underneath the navigation bar, and not take it with itself while scrolling. Fortunately for us, implementing this is extremely simple, just add a `fixed-top` class to the `navbar` element, as shown:

```
13    <body>
14      <nav class="navbar navbar-toggleable-md
        navbar-inverse bg-inverse fixed-top">
15        <button class="navbar-toggler navbar-toggler-right"
          type="button" d                  collapse" data-target="
          #navbarTogglerDemo              -controls="
          navbarTogglerDemo0              -expanded="false"
          aria-label="Tog         na      ation">
16          <span class      avbar-  oggler-icon"></span>
17        </button>
18
19        <a c      ="navbar-brand" href="index.php">
20            g src="http://res.cloudinary.com/sonarsystems/
              mage/upload/c_scale,w_150/v1442498022/
              Sonar-Systems-Circle-Logo_quet2k.png" width="30"
              height="30" alt="">
21        </a>
```

You may notice that the content of your website moves up slightly even when you are at the top of your website. Some of the content is behind the navigation bar; this is due to the `fixed-top` class making the navigation bar fixed, which means all other content will not flow relatively to the navigation bar. This can easily be fixed by inserting padding at the top of the content to push it all down. The amount of padding will vary depending on your navigation bar's height; for me, it's `56px`, and is most likely the same for you. This padding will be applied to the body using `padding-top`, as we want to push content from the top down. Add the following code to the `index.css` file:

```
1  body
2  {
3      padding-top: 56px;
4  }
```

Now when we run our website, the navigation bar will be fixed to the top while not hiding any content unless we scroll.

Changing the current button selected

In the navigation bar, we have two buttons. The **Home** button is always active/selected regardless of which of the buttons are pressed, this problem will also occur with more than two buttons. Let's implement some JavaScript to change the active status of the buttons when a button is actually pressed. By default, we will leave the **Home** button active on website launch.

If you go to the `HEADER.php` file, you will notice a class of `active` applied to the `Home` list item:

```
23    <div class="collapse navbar-collapse" id="
      navbarTogglerDemo02">
24      <ul class="navbar-nav mr-auto mt-2 mt-md-0">
25        <li class="nav-item active">
26          <a class="nav-link navButton" href="
            #HomeSection">Home <span class="sr-only">(
            current)</span></a>
27        </li>
28        <li class="nav-item">
29          <a class="nav-link navButton" href="#">Link</a
            >
30        </li>
31      </ul>
```

Add a class of `navLi` to all list items in the navigation bar, as follows:

```
23        <div class="collapse navbar-collapse" id="
          navbarTogglerDemo02">
24          <ul class="navbar-nav mr-auto mt-2 mt-md-0">
25            <li class="nav-item navLi active">
26              <a class="nav-link navButton" href="
                #HomeSection">Home <span class="sr-only">(
                current)</span></a>
27            </li>
28            <li class="nav-item navLi">
29              <a class="nav-link navButton" href="#">Link</a
                >
30            </li>
31          </ul>
```

The reason for us adding a new class instead of using the existing `nav-item` class is because your website may need `nav-item` elsewhere as it grows, which will cause conflicts.

Add the following code to the `index.js` file:

```
1   $( function( )
2   {
3       $( document ).on( 'click', '.navButton', function(
            event )
4       {
5           $( 'html, body' ).animate(
6           {
7               scrollTop: $( $( this ).attr('href') ).offset(
                    ).top
8           }, 200 );
9
10          event.preventDefault( );
11      } );
12
13      $( document ).on( 'click', '.navLi', function( event )
14      {
15          $( '.navLi' ).removeClass( 'active' );
16          $( this ).addClass( 'active' );
17      } );
18  } );
```

Let's run through each new line of code:

- **Line 1** removes the `active` class from all list items in the navigation bar
- **Line 2** adds the `active` class to the list item that was pressed by using the `this` keyword, which allows us to get the specific `nav` list item that was clicked

When clicking on another button in the navigation bar, it will highlight, as illustrated:

Common pitfalls

We have covered a lot in this chapter. Many of these things will serve as a basis for future projects within this book and beyond. Now we will look at some of the common problems you may face.

Navigation bar height variance on mobile devices

We implemented padding in our body to overcome the fact that the navigation bar, when fixed, was covering some of the content. Our current project works the same in this regard on all devices, but it is common for navigation bars to change size depending on the device/browser size. This can lead to the same problem; solving this can be done using media queries to check which device the website is running on.

Also, some websites may even change the size of the navigation bar on the same device/browser size. This can be due to the user scrolling and the navigation bar becoming smaller as a result. This can be very appealing visually, but media queries will be necessary to accommodate for this change.

Navigation bar button anchoring

You may have noticed, when clicking on the navigation buttons, that it doesn't work and provides an error similar to this:

```
⊗ ▶Uncaught TypeError: Cannot read property 'top' of undefined
      at HTMLAnchorElement.<anonymous> (index.js:7)
      at HTMLDocument.dispatch (jquery-3.2.1.min.js:3)
      at HTMLDocument.q.handle (jquery-3.2.1.min.js:3)

  >
```

This is due to the fact that the button is pointing to an element that doesn't exist. Any problems like this will be resolved as we/you naturally add the remaining sections to the website.

This isn't an exhaustive list of problems, so if you face any, feel free to reach out via my free education platform, at `http://www.sonarlearning.co.uk`

Summary

In this chapter, we covered creating our website's first section, linking it with our navigation bar, and modifying the website to accommodate this section. The next chapter will cover creating another section that can be reused over and over again.

5
Creating a Generic Reusable Single Page Section

This chapter will cover creating a generic section that can be extended to multiple sections. This section provides the ability to display any information your website needs. The importance of this chapter cannot be overstated: the majority of the sections in your single page website will be influenced by the skills learned in this chapter. They will allow you to create anything from a contact form to a pricing model.

The topics covered in this chapter are as follows:

- Generic single page section creation
- Anchoring this section to the overall single page website design flow
- Bootstrap images
- Bootstrap image grid layout
- Debugging and testing responsive design

Different sections in single page websites

There are countless variations when it comes to different sections that can be incorporated into the design of a single page website. In the previous chapter, we implemented an introduction section that contained a full width image and overlaying text. It is more than appropriate to have similar layouts for other sections, but let's look at some of the other commonly used layouts.

Single page sections are commonly used to display the following data to the user:

- Contact form (will be implemented in the next chapter).
- About us: This can be as simple as a couple of paragraphs talking about the company/individual or more complex with images, even showing the team and their roles.
- Projects/work: Any work you or the company has done and would like to showcase. They are usually linked to external pages or pop up boxes containing more information about the project.
- Useful company info such as opening times.

These are just some of the many uses for sections in a single page website. A good rule of thumb is that if it can be a page on another website it can most likely be adapted into sections on a single page website. Also, depending on the amount of information a single section has, it could potentially be split into multiple sections.

Single page section examples

Let's go through some examples of the sections mentioned.

Contact form

As can be seen by the contact form from Richman, the elements used are very similar to that of a contact page. A form is used with inputs for the various pieces of information required from the user along with a button for submission:

Not all contact forms will have the same fields. Put what you need, it may be more or less, there is no right or wrong answer. Also at the bottom of the section is the company's logo along with some written contact information, which is also very common. Some websites also display a map usually using the Google Maps API; these mainly have a physical presence such as a store.

Website link—http://richman-kcm.com/

About us

This is an excellent example of an about us page that uses the following elements to convey the information:

- **Images**: Display the individual's face. Creates a very personal touch to the otherwise digital website.
- **Title**: Used to display the individual's name. This can also be an image if you want a fancier title.
- **Simple text**: Talks about who the person is and what they do.
- **Icons**: Linking to the individual's social media accounts.

Website link—http://designedbyfew.com/

Projects/work

This website shows its work off very elegantly and cleanly using images and little text:

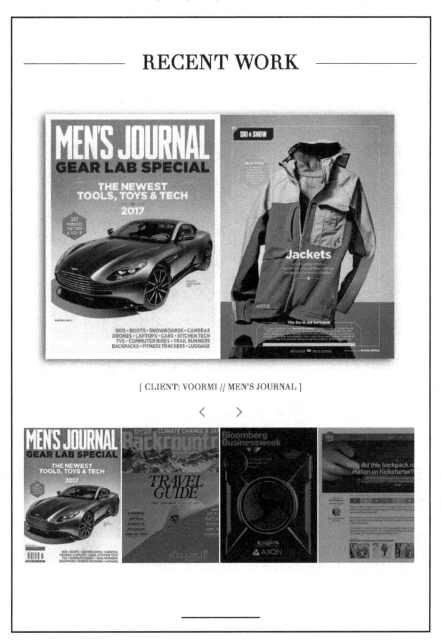

It also provides a carousel-like slider to display the work, which is extremely useful for displaying the content bigger without displaying all of it at once and it allows a lot of content for a small section to be used.

Website link: `http://peeltheorange.com/#recent-work`

Opening times

This website uses a background image similar to the introduction section created in the previous chapter and an additional image on top to display the opening times.

This can also be achieved using a mixture of text and CSS styling for various facets such as the border.

Website link—`http://www.mumbaigate.co.uk/`

Implementing our generic reusable single page section

We will now create a generic section that can easily be modified and reused to our single page portfolio website. But we still need some sort of layout/design in mind before we implement the section, let's go with an *Our Team* style section.

What will the Our Team section contain?

The *Our Team* section will be a bit simpler than the examples shown earlier in this chapter, but it can easily be modified to accommodate the animations and styles displayed on the previously mentioned websites. It will be similar to the following example:

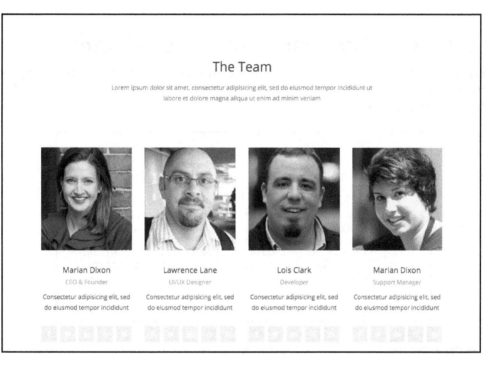

Website link—http://demo.themeum.com/html/oxygen/

The preceding example consists of the following elements:

- Heading
- Intro text (Lorem Ipsum in this case)
- Images displaying each member of the team
- Team member's name
- Their role
- Text informing the viewer a little bit about them
- Social links

We will also create our section using a similar layout. We are now finally going to use the column system to its full potential to provide a responsive experience using breakpoints. I would recommend going to the previous example and resizing your browser to see how the section reacts. I would recommend doing this on all the examples from this book as it will help you understand the common design decisions that most websites adhere to.

Creating the Our Team section container

First let's implement a simple container, with the title and section introduction text, without any extra elements such as an image. We will then use this to link to our navigation bar. Add the following code to the jumbotron `div`:

```
 9  <div class="container-fluid" id="TeamSection">
10    <div class="row">
11      <div class="col-12 text-center">
12        <h1>Our Awesome Team</h1>
13
14        <p>
15          Lorem ipsum dolor sit amet, consectetur
             adipiscing elit, sed do eiusmod tempor incididunt
             ut labore et dolore magna aliqua. Ut enim ad
             minim veniam, quis nostrud exercitation ullamco
             laboris nisi ut aliquip ex ea commodo consequat.
16        </p>
17      </div>
18    </div>
19  </div>
```

Let's go over what the preceding code is doing:

- **Line 9** creates a container that is fluid, allowing it to span the browser's width fully. This can be changed to a regular container if you like. The `id` will be used very soon to link to the navigation bar.
- **Line 10** creates a row in which our text elements will be stored.
- **Line 11** creates a `div` that spans all the 12 columns on all screen sizes and centers the text inside of it.
- **Line 12** creates a simple header for the Team section.
- **Line 14** to **Line 16** adds introduction text. I have put the first two sentences of "Lorem Ipsum..." inside of it, but you can put anything you like.

All of this produces the following result:

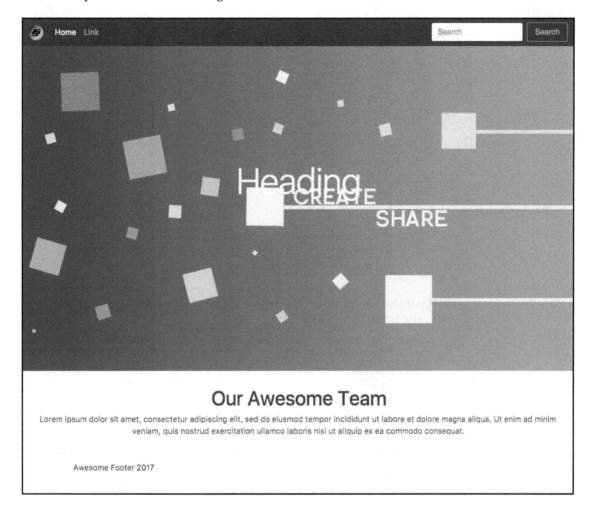

Anchoring the Team section to the navigation bar

As we did in the previous chapter, we will now link the navigation bar to the Team section. This will allow the user to navigate to the Team section without having to scroll up or down. At the moment, there is no need to scroll up, but when more content is added this can become a problem as a single page website can become quite long. Fortunately, we have already done the heavy lifting with the navigation bar through HTML and JavaScript, phew!

First, let's change the name of the second button in the navigation bar to `Team`. Update the navigation bar like so:

```
23      <div class="collapse navbar-collapse" id="
        navbarTogglerDemo02">
24        <ul class="navbar-nav mr-auto mt-2 mt-md-0">
25          <li class="nav-item navLi active">
26            <a class="nav-link navButton" href="
              #HomeSection">Home <span class="sr-only">(
              current)</span></a>
27          /li>
28          li class="nav-item navLi">
29            <a class="nav-link navButton" href="#">Team</a
              >
30          </li>
31        </ul>
```

The navigation bar will now look as follows:

Fantastic, our navigation bar is looking more like what you would see on a real website. Now let's change `href` to the same ID as the Team section, which was `#TeamSection` like so:

```
23      <div class="collapse navbar-collapse" id="
        navbarTogglerDemo02">
24        <ul class="navbar-nav mr-auto mt-2 mt-md-0">
25          <li class="nav-item navLi active">
26            <a class="nav-link navButton" href="
              #HomeSection">Home <span class="sr-only">(
              current)</span></a>
27          </li>
28          <li class="nav-item navLi">
29            <a class="nav-link navButton" href="
              #TeamSection">Team</a>
30          </li>
31        </ul>
```

Now when we click on any of the navigation buttons we get no JavaScript errors like we would have in the previous chapter. Also, it automatically scrolls to each section without any extra JavaScript code.

Adding the team's pictures

Now let's use images to showcase the team members. I will use the image from the following link for our employees, but in a real website you would obviously use different images:

`http://res.cloudinary.com/dmliyxggm/image/upload/v1511699813/John_vepwoz.png`

I have modified the image so all the background is removed and the image is trimmed, so it looks as follows:

Up until now, all images that we have used have been stored on other websites such as CDN's, this is great, but the need may arise when the use of a custom image like the previous one is needed. We can either store it on a CDN, which is a very good approach, and I would recommend Cloudinary (`http://cloudinary.com/`), or we can store it locally, which we will do now.

> A **CDN** is a **Content Delivery Network** that has a sole purpose of delivering content such as images to other websites using the best and fastest servers available to a specific user. I would definitely recommend using one.

Create a folder called `Images` and place the image using the following folder structure:

- Root
    - CSS
    - Images
        - Team
            - Thumbnails
                - Thumbnails.png
    - Index.php
    - JS
    - SNIPPETS

This may seem like overkill, considering we only have one image, but as your website gets more complex you will store more images and having an intelligent folder structure/hierarchy will save an immense amount of time.

Add the following code to the first row like so:

```
 9  <div class="container-fluid" id="TeamSection">
10    <div class="row">
11      <div class="col-12 text-center">
12        <h1>Our Awesome Team</h1>
13
14        <p>
15          Lorem ipsum dolor sit amet, consectetur
             adipiscing elit, sed do eiusmod tempor incididunt
             ut labore et dolore magna aliqua. Ut enim ad
             minim veniam, quis nostrud exercitation ullamco
             laboris nisi ut aliquip ex ea commodo consequat.
16        </p>
17      </div>
18    </div>
19
20    <div class="row">
21      <div class="col-lg-3 col-sm-6 col-xs-12">
22      </div>
23
24      <div class="col-lg-3 col-sm-6 col-xs-12">
25      </div>
26
27      <div class="col-lg-3 col-sm-6 col-xs-12">
28      </div>
29
30      <div class="col-lg-3 col-sm-6 col-xs-12">
31      </div>
32    </div>
33  </div>
```

The code we have added doesn't actually provide any visual changes as it is nothing but empty `div` classes. But these `div` classes will serve as structures for each team member and their respective content such as name and social links.

We created a new row to group our new `div` classes. Inside each `div` we will represent each team member. The classes have been set up to be displayed like so:

- Extra small screens will only show a single team member on a single row
- Small and medium screens will show two team members on a single row
- Large and extra large screens will show four team members on a single row

The rows are rows in their literal sense and not the class row. Another way to look at them is as lines.

The sizes/breakpoints can easily be changed using the information regarding the grid from Chapter 2, *What Is Bootstrap, Why Do We Use It?*

Now let's add the team's images, update the previous code like so:

```
 9  <div class="container-fluid" id="TeamSection">
10    <div class="row">
11      <div class="col-12 text-center">
12        <h1>Our Awesome Team</h1>
13
14        <p>
15          Lorem ipsum dolor sit amet, consectetur
             adipiscing elit, sed do eiusmod tempor incididunt
             ut labore et dolore magna aliqua. Ut enim ad
             minim veniam, quis nostrud exercitation ullamco
             laboris nisi ut aliquip ex ea commodo consequat.
16        </p>
17      </div>
18    </div>
19
20    <div class="row">
21      <div class="col-lg-3 col-sm-6 col-xs-12">
22        <img src="Images/Team/Thumbnails/Thumbnail.png" />
23      </div>
24
25      <div class="col-lg-3 col-sm-6 col-xs-12">
26        <img src="Images/Team/Thumbnails/Thumbnail.png" />
27      </div>
28
29      <div class="col-lg-3 col-sm-6 col-xs-12">
30        <img src="Images/Team/Thumbnails/Thumbnail.png" />
31      </div>
32
33      <div class="col-lg-3 col-sm-6 col-xs-12">
34        <img src="Images/Team/Thumbnails/Thumbnail.png" />
35      </div>
36    </div>
37  </div>
```

The preceding code produces the following result:

As you can see, this is not the desired effect we were looking for. As there are no size restrictions on the image, it is displayed at its original size. Which, on some screens, will produce a result similar to the monstrosity you see before you; worry not, this can easily be fixed.

Add the classes `img-fluid` and `img-thumbnail` to each one of the images like so:

```
20    <div class="row">
21      <div class="col-lg-3 col-sm-6 col-xs-12">
22        <img src="Images/Team/Thumbnails/Thumbnail.png"
          class="img-fluid img-thumbnail" />
23      </div>
24
25      <div class="col-lg-3 col-sm-6 col-xs-12">
26        <img src="Images/Team/Thumbnails/Thumbnail.png"
          class="img-fluid img-thumbnail" />
27      </div>
28
29      <div class="col-lg-3 col-sm-6 col-xs-12">
30        <img src="Images/Team/Thumbnails/Thumbnail.png"
          class="img-fluid img-thumbnail" />
31      </div>
32
33      <div class="col-lg-3 col-sm-6 col-xs-12">
34        <img src="Images/Team/Thumbnails/Thumbnail.png"
          class="img-fluid img-thumbnail" />
35      </div>
36    </div>
37  </div>
```

The classes we added are designed to provide the following styling:

- `img-fluid`: Provides a responsive image that is automatically restricted based on the number of columns and browser size.
- `img-thumbnail`: Is more of an optional class, but it is still very useful. It provides a light border around the images to make them pop.

This produces the following result:

As can be seen, this is significantly better than our previous result. Depending on the browser/screen size, the positioning will slightly change based on the column breakpoints we specified. As usual, I recommend that you resize the browser to see the different layouts.

These images are almost complete; they look fine on most screen sizes, but they aren't actually centered within their respective `div`. This is evident on larger screen sizes, as can be seen here:

It isn't very noticeable, but the problem is there, it can be seen to the right of the last image. You probably could get away without fixing this, but when creating anything, from a website to a game, or even a table, the smallest details are what separate the good websites from the amazing websites. This is a simple idea called the **aggregation of marginal gains**. Fortunately for us, like many times before, Bootstrap offers functionality to resolve our little problem. Simply add the `text-center` class, to the row within the `div` of the images like so:

```
19
20    <div class="row text-center">
21        <div class="col-lg-3 col-sm-6 col-xs-12">
22            <img src="Images/Team/Thumbnails/Thumbnail.png"
              class="img-fluid img-thumbnail" />
23        </div>
24
25        <div class="col-lg-3 col-sm-6 col-xs-12">
26            <img src="Images/Team/Thumbnails/Thumbnail.png"
              class="img-fluid img-thumbnail" />
27        </div>
28
29        <div class="col-lg-3 col-sm-6 col-xs-12">
30            <img src="Images/Team/Thumbnails/Thumbnail.png"
              class="img-fluid img-thumbnail" />
31        </div>
32
33        <div class="col-lg-3 col-sm-6 col-xs-12">
34            <img src="Images/Team/Thumbnails/Thumbnail.png"
              class="img-fluid img-thumbnail" />
35        </div>
36    </div>
```

This now produces the following result:

There is one more slight problem that is only noticeable on smaller screens when the images/member containers are stacked on top of each other. The following result is produced:

The problem might not jump out at first glance, but look closely to the gaps between the images that are stacked, or I should say, to the lack of a gap. This isn't the end of the world, but again the small details make an immense difference to the look of a website. This can be easily fixed by adding padding to each team member `div`. First add a class of `teamMemberContainer` to each team member `div` like so:

```
20    <div class="row text-center">
21      <div class="col-lg-3 col-sm-6 col-xs-12
        teamMemberContainer">
22          <img src="Images/Team/Thumbnails/Thumbnail.png"
            class="img-fluid img-thumbnail" />
23      </div>
24
25      <div class="col-lg-3 col-sm-6 col-xs-12
        teamMemberContainer">
26          <img src="Images/Team/Thumbnails/Thumbnail.png"
            class="img-fluid img-thumbnail" />
27      </div>
28
29      <div class="col-lg-3 col-sm-6 col-xs-12
        teamMemberContainer">
30          <img src="Images/Team/Thumbnails/Thumbnail.png"
            class="img-fluid img-thumbnail" />
31      </div>
32
33      <div class="col-lg-3 col-sm-6 col-xs-12
        teamMemberContainer">
34          <img src="Images/Team/Thumbnails/Thumbnail.png"
            class="img-fluid img-thumbnail" />
35      </div>
36    </div>
```

Add the following CSS code to the `index.css` file to provide a more visible gap through the use of padding:

```
29  .teamMemberContainer
30  {
31      padding: 5px;
32  }
```

This simple solution now produces the following result:

If you want the gap to be bigger, simply increase the value and lower it to reduce the gap.

Team member info text

The previous section covered quite a lot, if you're not 100% on what we did just go back and take a second look. This section will thankfully be very simple as it will incorporate techniques and features we have already covered, to add the following information to each team member:

- Name
- Job title
- Member info text
- Plus anything else you need

Update each team member container with the following code:

```
21   <div class="col-lg-3 col-sm-6 col-xs-12
     teamMemberContainer">
22     <img src="Images/Team/Thumbnails/Thumbnail.png"
       class="img-fluid img-thumbnail" />
23
24     <h4>John</h4>
25
26     <p class="text-muted">Protagonist</p>
27
28     <p>John is the most awesome person in the world.</p>
29   </div>
```

Let's go over the new code line by line:

- **Line 24** adds a simple header that is intended to display the team member's name. I have chosen an h4 tag, but you can use something bigger or smaller if you like.
- **Line 26** adds the team member's job title, I have used a paragraph element with the Bootstrap class text-muted, which lightens the text color. If you would like more information regarding text styling within Bootstrap, feel free to check out the following link.
- **Line 28** adds a simple paragraph with no extra styling to display some information about the team member.

Bootstrap text styling link—https://v4-alpha.getbootstrap.com/ utilities/colors/

The code that we just added will produce the following result:

As usual, resize your browser to simulate different screen sizes. I use Chrome as my main browser, but Safari has an awesome feature baked right in that allows you to see how your website will run on different browsers/devices, this link will help you use this feature—https://www.tekrevue.com/tip/safari-responsive-design-mode/ Most browsers have a plethora of plugins to aid in this process, but not only does Safari have it built in, it works really well.

It all looks fantastic, but again I will nitpick at the gaps. The image is right on top of the team member name text; a small gap would really help improve the visual fidelity. Add a class of `teamMemberImage` to each image tag as it is demonstrated here:

```
21    <div class="col-lg-3 col-sm-6 col-xs-12
      teamMemberContainer">
22      <img src="Images/Team/Thumbnails/Thumbnail.png"
      class="img-fluid img-thumbnail teamMemberImage" />
23
24      <h4>John</h4>
25
26      <p class="text-muted">Protagonist</p>
27
28      <p>John is the most awesome person in the world.</p>
29    </div>
```

Now add the following code to the `index.css` file, which will apply a margin of `10px` below the image, hence moving all the content down:

```
34  .teamMemberImage
35  {
36      margin-bottom: 10px;
37  }
```

Change the margin to suit your needs.

This very simple code will produce the following similar yet subtly different and more visually appealing result:

Team member social links

We have almost completed the Team section, only the social links remain for each team member. I will be using simple images for the social buttons from the following link:

`https://simplesharebuttons.com/html-share-buttons/`

I will also only be adding three social icons, but feel free to add as many or as few as you need. Add the following code to the button of each team member container:

```
20    <div class="row text-center">
21      <div class="col-lg-3 col-sm-6 col-xs-12
        teamMemberContainer">
22        <img src="Images/Team/Thumbnails/Thumbnail.png"
          class="img-fluid img-thumbnail teamMemberImage" />
23
24        <h4>John</h4>
25
26        <p class="text-muted">Protagonist</p>
27
28        <p>John is the most awesome person in the world.</p>
29
30        <div class="col-12">
31          <a href="" target="_blank">
32            <img class="socialImages" src="https://
             simplesharebuttons.com/images/somacro/
             facebook.png" alt="Facebook" />
33          </a>
34
35          <a href="" target="_blank">
36            <img class="socialImages" src="https://
             simplesharebuttons.com/images/somacro/
             google.png" alt="Google" />
37          </a>
38
39          <a href="" target="_blank">
40            <img class="socialImages" src="https://
             simplesharebuttons.com/images/somacro/
             twitter.png" alt="Twitter" />
41          </a>
42        </div>
43      </div>
```

Let's go over each new line of code:

- **Line 30** creates a `div` to store all the social buttons for each team member
- **Line 31** creates a link to Facebook (add your social link in the `href`)
- **Line 32** adds an image to show the Facebook social link
- **Line 35** creates a link to Google+ (add your social link in the `href`)
- **Line 36** adds an image to show the Google+ social link
- **Line 39** creates a link to Twitter (add your social link in the `href`)
- **Line 40** adds an image to show the Twitter social link

We have added a class that needs to be implemented, but let's first run our website to see the result without any styling:

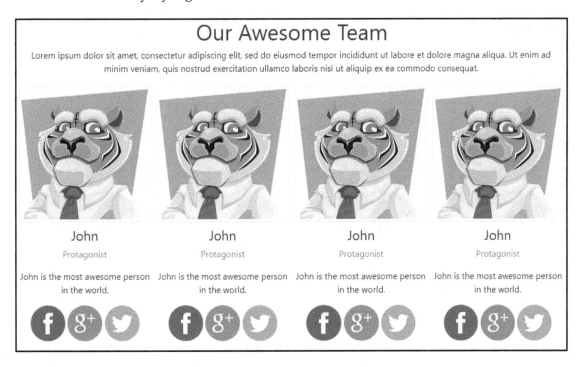

It looks OK, but the social icons are a bit big, especially if we were to have more icons. Add the following CSS styling to the index.css file:

```
39 .socialImages
40 {
41     width: 50px;
42 }
```

This piece of code simply restricts the social icons size to 50px. Only setting the width causes the height to be automatically calculated, this ensures that any changes to the image that involves a ratio change won't mess up the look of the icons. This now produces the following result:

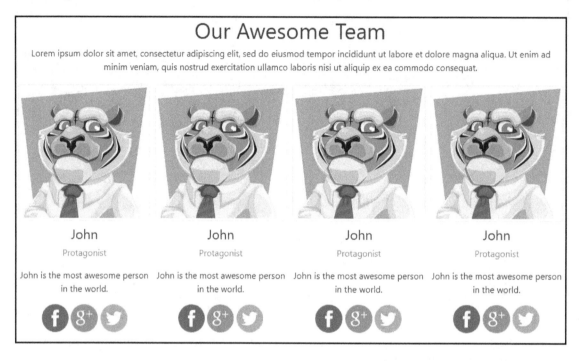

Feel free to change width to suit your desires. With the social buttons implemented we are done.

Summary

In this chapter, we covered implementing another section to our single page website to showcase team members. We now have a solid base for more sections as and when our website needs them. The next chapter will cover adding the final section to our website, providing a contact form.

6
Creating a Contact Us Section

This chapter will cover adding another section to our single page website that can be extended to multiple sections. This section will display a contact form, but it can easily be adapted to provide information to the user, as we have discussed in previous chapters.

The topics covered in this chapter are as follows:

- Anchoring the section to the overall single page website design flow
- Bootstrap/HTML forms
- Bootstrap/HTML single line text input
- Bootstrap/HTML multiline text input
- Bootstrap/HTML button input
- Responsive forms
- Debugging and testing responsive design

Contact Us examples for single page websites

Though contact forms come in a variety of shapes and sizes, the majority of them use the same tried and tested layout, which are usually of the following:

- Name input field
- Email address input field
- Message/description multi line text field
- Send button

Other sections can be added, but most contact forms will resemble the preceding listed components.

There are countless variations when it comes to different sections that the single page website can display. In Chapter 4, *Creating the Introduction Section* we implemented an introduction section that contained a full width image and overlaying text. It is more than appropriate to have similar layouts for other sections, but let's look at some of the other commonly used layouts.

Let's go through some contact form examples.

Richman

This example is the same one we looked at in the previous section and it is simple yet very effective in conveying to the user what information is required for submitting a query.

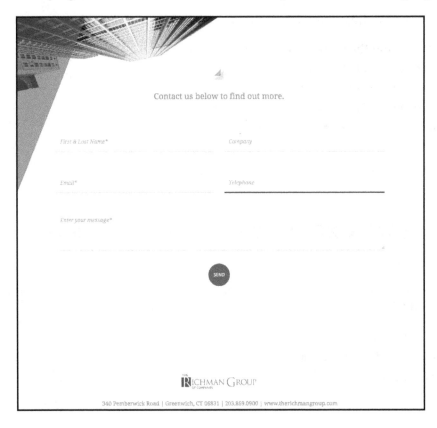

Even though the fields are slightly different to the ones listed in the previous section, they essentially require the same information, which again is:

- Who you are
- How to get in touch with you
- Your query

Website link—`http://richman-kcm.com/`

Bueno

This example is simpler and contains the exact components we mentioned earlier in this chapter:

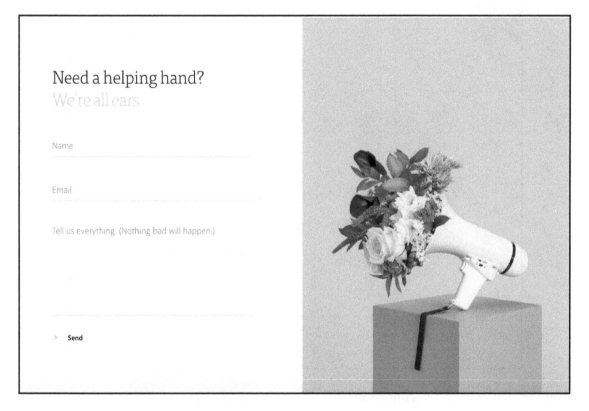

There is also an image to complement the contact form.

Website link: `https://bueno.co/#contact`

This also

This example is totally different in that it has no contact form, but it provides details on where they can be found **in real life** (IRL).

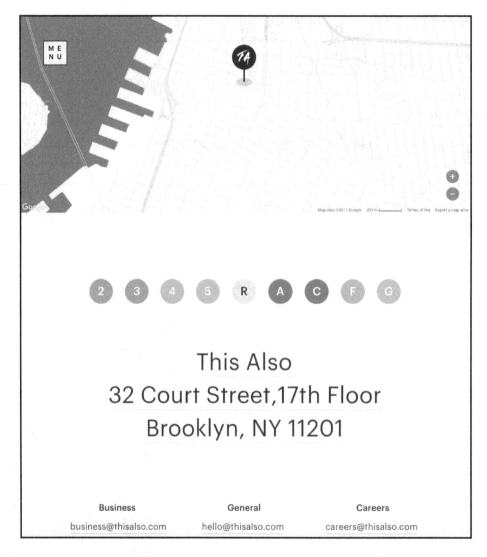

It also provides the email address for different departments along with a map.

Website link—http://thisalso.com/contact

Design museum

This is another example with no contact form, just simple contact details along with a map, but this time using the Google Maps API, which is free, extremely powerful and familiar.

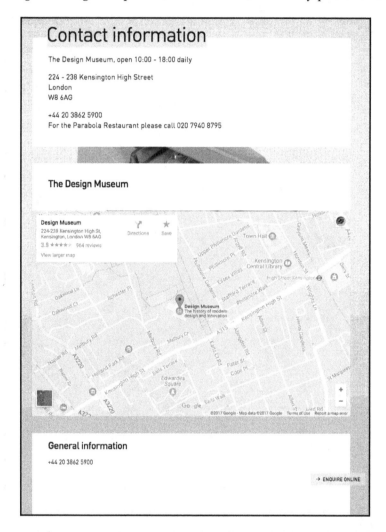

If you scroll down there are more departments that can be contacted.

Website link—http://designmuseum.org/plan-your-visit/contact-information

Choice screening

Though this example is similar to the first two in that there is a contact form with fields to fill out, there is a lot more information required and that isn't a bad thing.

Depending on the nature of your business, your contact form will be reflective of this.

Website link—https://www.choicescreening.com/contact-choice-screening

Implementing the Contact Us section

We will now create a Contact Us section that can easily be modified and reused for our Single Page Portfolio website.

What will the Contact Us section contain?

The Contact Us section will be very similar to the previous Richman and Bueno examples, but it can easily be adapted to the other website styles.

The Contact Us section will consist of the following elements:

- Name input using a single line input field
- Email address input using a single line input field
- Message/description input using a multiline input field

We will incorporate many of the techniques covered in previous chapters, including the awesome grid system, courtesy of Bootstrap. Before moving on with this chapter, I would recommend checking out all the examples we discussed previously and resizing the web browser to see how they react to responsive design.

Creating the Contact Us section container

First let's implement a simple container that will hold our contact form. We will then use this to link to our navigation bar. Add the following code below the our `Team` section:

```
119  <div class="container-fluid" id="ContactSection">
120    <div class="row">
121      <div class="col-12 text-center">
122        <h1>Contact Us</h1>
123      </div>
124    </div>
125  </div>
```

Let's go over what the preceding code is doing:

- **Line 119** creates a container that is fluid, allowing it to span the browser's width fully. This can be changed to a regular container if you like. The ID will be used very soon to link to the navigation bar.
- **Line 120** creates a row in which our elements will be stored.

- **Line 121** creates a div that spans all the 12 columns on all screen sizes and centers the text inside of it.
- **Line 122** creates a simple header for the Contact Us section.

The preceding code that we added to our website produces the following result:

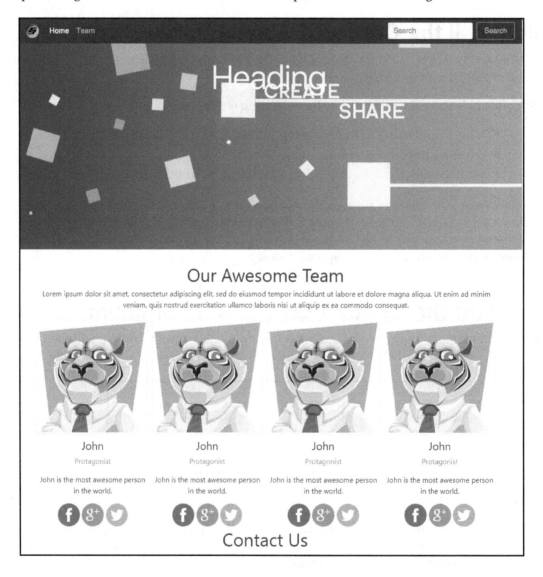

The Contact Us section blends in with the team section as they have the same background color. It is very common for single page websites to have different background colors/images for each section. One very popular method is to alternate between dark and light backgrounds. The team section already has a white background, let's make the Contact Us section black.

Add the following styling code to the `index.css` file:

```
44  #ContactSection
45▾ {
46      background-color: #000000;
47      color: #FFFFFF;
48  }
```

Let's go over what the preceding code is doing:

- **Line 45** sets the background color of the Contact Us section to black
- **Line 46** sets the text color of the content inside the Contact Us section to white

This will invert the colors as shown as follows:

You may notice that the Contact Us header has less space at the top compared to the team header. This is due to the fact that a jumbotron in Bootstrap has a margin automatically applied, let's apply something very similar to all the other sections.

Update the CSS code we previously added to include a margin and border at the top and bottom of the Contact Us section:

```
44  #ContactSection
45  {
46      background-color: #000000;
47      color: #FFFFFF;
48      margin-top: 2rem;
49      margin-bottom: 2rem;
50      padding-top: 2rem;
51      padding-bottom: 2rem;
52  }
```

I have chosen `2rem` as that is what the jumbotron applies, but you can modify this value as you see fit. This now produces the following result:

Anchoring the Contact Us section to the navigation bar

Similar to the previous chapter, we will link the navigation bar to the Contact Us section. This will allow the user to navigate to the Contact Us section without having to scroll up or down.

There are only two items in the navigation bar, which have already been assigned to the introduction and team section, respectively. We will need to create a whole new item and add the following code to the existing navigation bar items:

```
23      <div class="collapse navbar-collapse" id="
        navbarTogglerDemo02">
24        <ul class="navbar-nav mr-auto mt-2 mt-md-0">
25          <li class="nav-item navLi active">
26            <a class="nav-link navButton" href="
              #HomeSection">Home <span class="sr-only">(
              current)</span></a>
27          </li>
28
29          <li class="nav-item navLi">
30            <a class="nav-link navButton" href="
              #TeamSection">Team</a>
31          </li>
32
33          <li class="nav-item navLi">
34            <a class="nav-link navButton" href="
              #ContactSection">Contact Us</a>
35          </li>
36        </ul>
```

This now anchors the navigation bar to our Contact Us section and adds a new menu item as follows:

It automatically scrolls beautifully to the Contact Us section with the JavaScript we added earlier in this chapter.

Adding the contact form

Now let's add some input fields for the contact form, we will start off with the following:

- **Email address**: Single line input field
- **Name**: Single line input field

 A single line input field is one that only allows a single line of text as the name suggests, this is great for simple data such as the previously shown data.

Add the following code to the header row that we implemented in the previous section:

```
119  <div class="container-fluid" id="ContactSection">
120    <div class="row">
121      <div class="col-12 text-center">
122        <h1>Contact Us</h1>
123      </div>
124    </div>
125
126    <form>
127      <div class="row">
128        <div>
129          <label for="contactEmail">Email address</label>
130          <input type="email" class="form-control" id="
             contactEmail" placeholder="Enter email address">
131          <small class="form-text">We'll never share your
             email with anyone else.</small>
132        </div>
133
134        <div>
135          <label for="contactName">Name</label>
136          <input type="text" class="form-control" id="
             contactName" placeholder="Name">
137        </div>
138      </div>
139    </form>
140  </div>
```

Let's run through the code we added line by line:

- **Line 126** adds a form that will contain all of the contact form elements. This can easily be extended with a form action to create a fully functioning contact form with the aid of a back-end server using a server language such as PHP.
- **Line 127** creates a row for all of our contact form elements to reside in. Nothing special here, we have done this a million and one times already.
- **Line 128** creates a `div` that will contain all the email address elements.
- **Line 129** adds a label to inform the user that this field is for their email address.
- **Line 130** adds an email input field with email validation.
- **Line 131** creates some small text to reassure the user that their email address will be kept confidential.
- **Line 134** creates a `div` that will contain all the name elements.
- **Line 135** adds a label to inform the user that this field is for their name.
- **Line 136** adds a text input field for the name.

All of this produces the following result:

Before we add the rest of the contact form elements, you're most likely thinking to yourself that this does not look like the examples we looked at earlier, you're absolutely right. It doesn't fully make use of the space available. Lucky for us, all we have to do is add column classes to each `div` containing the different elements like so:

```
126    <form>
127      <div class="row">
128        <div class="col-md-6">
129          <label for="contactEmail">Email address</label>
130          <input type="email" class="form-control" id="
               contactEmail" placeholder="Enter email address">
131          <small class="form-text">We'll never share your
               email with anyone else.</small>
132        </div>
133
134        <div class="col-md-6">
135          <label for="contactName">Name</label>
136          <input type="text" class="form-control" id="
               contactName" placeholder="Name">
137        </div>
138      </div>
139    </form>
```

This forces the inputs to be half the width of the row on devices that are medium size or bigger and on a single row for small and extra small sizes.

On larger devices it will appear like this:

On smaller devices it will appear like this:

Our contact form is coming together nicely, add the following code to implement a message multiline input field:

```
126    <form>
127      <div class="row">
128        <div class="col-md-6">
129          <label for="contactEmail">Email address</label>
130          <input type="email" class="form-control" id="
                contactEmail" placeholder="Enter email address">
131          <small class="form-text">We'll never share your
                email with anyone else.</small>
132        </div>
133
134        <div class="col-md-6">
135          <label for="contactName">Name</label>
136          <input type="text" class="form-control" id="
                contactName" placeholder="Name">
137        </div>
138
139        <div class="col-12">
140          <label for="contactMessage">Message</label>
141          <textarea class="form-control" id="contactMessage
                " rows="5"></textarea>
142        </div>
143      </div>
144    </form>
```

Producing the following:

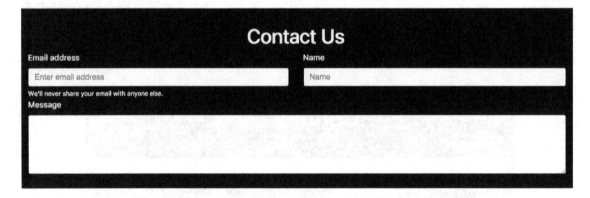

The last element to add is the send button, which can be easily added using the following code:

```
126    <form>
127      <div class="row">
128        <div class="col-md-6">
129          <label for="contactEmail">Email address</label>
130          <input type="email" class="form-control" id="
             contactEmail" placeholder="Enter email address">
131          <small class="form-text">We'll never share your
             email with anyone else.</small>
132        </div>
133
134        <div class="col-md-6">
135          <label for="contactName">Name</label>
136          <input type="text" class="form-control" id="
             contactName" placeholder="Name">
137        </div>
138
139        <div class="col-12">
140          <label for="contactMessage">Message</label>
141          <textarea class="form-control" id="contactMessage
             " rows="5"></textarea>
142        </div>
143
144        <div class="col-12">
145          <button type="submit" class="btn btn-primary
             col-12">Send Message</button>
146        </div>
147      </div>
148    </form>
```

Let's go over the button code line by line:

- **Line 144** simply creates a div to contain the button
- **Line 145** creates a button incorporating built-in Bootstrap classes for styling and spans 12 columns (full width of the parent container)

> More information about buttons and styling them with Bootstrap is situated here https://v4-alpha.getbootstrap.com/components/buttons/

This will produce the following result:

It's looking good, but not great, adding a gap between the message text area element and the send button will help improve the visual fidelity of the contact form. First add an ID of ContactButtonContainer to the button parent div like so:

```
126    <form>
127      <div class="row">
128        <div class="col-md-6">
129          <label for="contactEmail">Email address</label>
130          <input type="email" class="form-control" id="
             contactEmail" placeholder="Enter email address">
131          <small class="form-text">We'll never share your
             email with anyone else.</small>
132        </div>
133
134        <div class="col-md-6">
135          <label for="contactName">Name</label>
136          <input type="text" class="form-control" id="
             contactName" placeholder="Name">
137        </div>
138
139        <div class="col-12">
140          <label for="contactMessage">Message</label>
141          <textarea class="form-control" id="contactMessage
             " rows="5"></textarea>
142        </div>
143
144        <div class="col-12" id="ContactButtonContainer">
145          <button type="submit" class="btn btn-primary
             col-12">Send Message</button>
146        </div>
147      </div>
148    </form>
```

Visually, the website will remain the same as before unless we add some styles for this `div`. This can be achieved by adding the following code to the `index.css` file:

```
54 #ContactButtonContainer
55 {
56     margin-top: 10px;
57 }
```

Which in turn produces this awesome result:

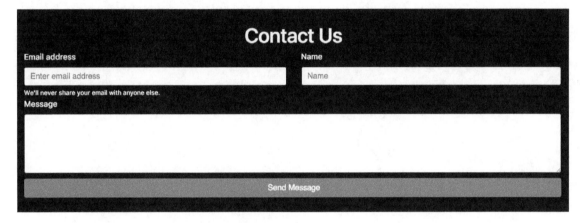

We are now done with the contact form section and also the single page website.

Summary

In this chapter, we created a new section for the contact form and added it to our single page website. The next chapter will kick start our next project, which is to create a blog.

7
Creating the Blog Posts Home Page

This chapter will start off our next project, which will be a blog. This time round our website will consist of two pages instead of a single page. In this chapter, we will design and implement the home page of the blog, which will display all the blog posts to the user in a simple and concise format.

The topics covered in this chapter are as follows:

- Bootstrap cards
- Bootstrap sections
- HTML images
- CSS text colors
- CSS fonts
- HTML page anchor tags
- Debugging and testing responsive design

Blog examples

As always, looking at other people's work is a great way of formulating the foundations of a product, be it a website or a chair. We aren't going to look at any chairs, but let's take a look at some blogs (you can try and find some blogs about chairs) and see their design decisions.

Let's go through some contact form examples.

TechCrunch

TechCrunch is a fantastic example of a classic tried and tested tabloid style brought to the modern age. There are various elements from images, to videos to text, and much much more.

Website link: https://techcrunch.com/

Gawker

Gawker is simpler, but it provides the blog posts in a clean linear format that is easily accessible on all devices.

Website link: `http://gawker.com/`

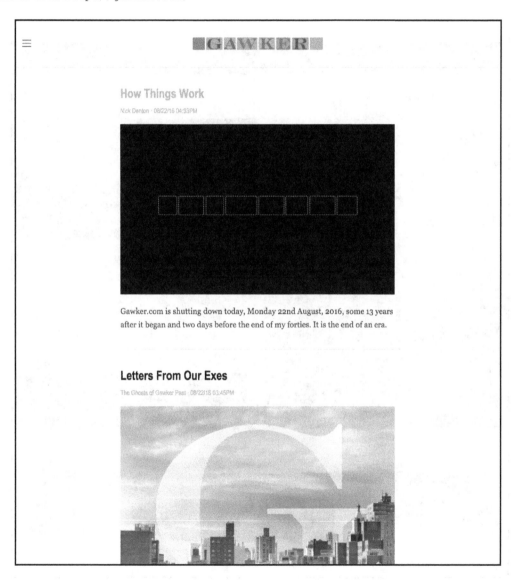

Microsoft News

Microsoft News is a nice blend of classic tabloid and modern flat design, in many ways it is simple but so effective.

Website link: https://news.microsoft.com/stories/

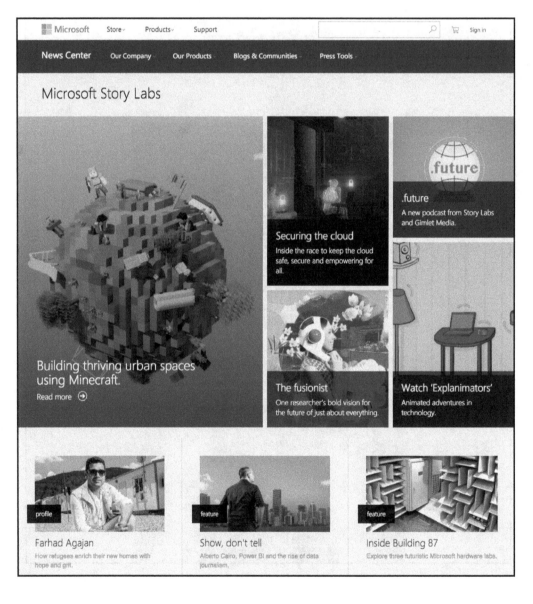

Johnny Cupcakes

Johnny Cupcakes isn't a website that is widely known, but it should definitely be on any list of innovative and modern designs. The blog uses scrolling to dynamically change the background image for different blog posts.

Website link: `http://kitchen.johnnycupcakes.com/`

TESCO Living

TESCO's blog is similar to Microsoft's, but it uses a really big image slider/carousel that helps highlight the company's latest and greatest.

Website link: `https://www.tescoliving.com/`

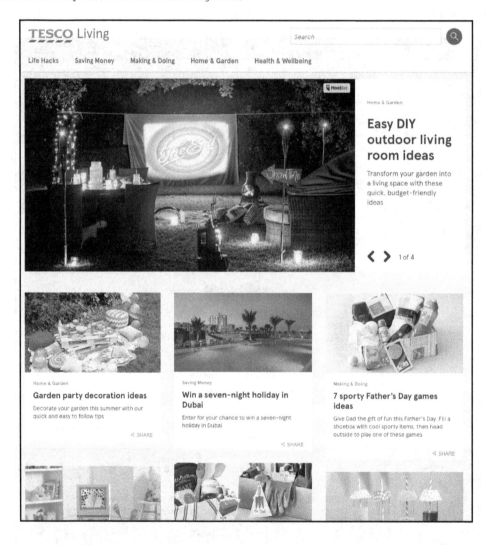

Setting up the base project

We could start with the Reusable Project Template that we created back in Chapter 3, *Reusable Project Template*, which would be more than adequate. Most of the additions from project 1 (single page website) are no longer needed, but some are generic such as the creation of a JavaScript file. So we will go through the code from the end of the previous chapter and refactor it to suit the blog that will be implemented over the next two chapters.

Removing all unnecessary files

Let's start by removing all files that are no longer needed due to them being specific to the single page project. The only files that we need to completely remove from our project are the image files, so remove all files/folders from the Images folder, the new structure should look as follows:

- Root
  - CSS
    - css
  - Images (empty folder)
  - php
  - JS
    - js
  - SNIPPETS
    - php
    - php

Refactoring the index.css file

Now let's remove all code from the index.css file that was added purposely for the single page website. This will be very simple, remove all code other than the styling applied to the body, only the following code should remain:

```
1 body
2 {
3     padding-top: 56px;
4 }
```

Refactoring the index.php file

Now let's remove all unneeded code from the `index.php` file. Again, this is very simple, remove all HTML code that is between the PHP `require_once` lines of your `index.php` file, it should resemble the following:

```
1  <?php require_once( "SNIPPETS/HEADER.php" ); ?>
2
3  |
4
5  <?php require_once( "SNIPPETS/FOOTER.php" ); ?>
```

Refactoring the HEADER.php snippet file

The `HEADER.php` file for the most part will remain untouched. The only change we will make is to remove the navigation buttons as the navigation bar will only allow the user to go to the home page. This can be achieved by clicking the image/logo in the navigation bar. Remove the following code:

```
23    <div class="collapse navbar-collapse" id="
      navbarTogglerDemo02">
24        <ul class="navbar-nav mr-auto mt-2 mt-md-0">
25            <li class="nav-item navLi active">
26              <a class="nav-link navButton" href="
                #HomeSection">Home <span class="sr-only">(
                current)</span></a>
27            </li>
28
29            <li class="nav-item navLi">
30              <a class="nav-link navButton" href="
                #TeamSection">Team</a>
31            </li>
32
33            <li class="nav-item navLi">
34              <a class="nav-link navButton" href="
                #ContactSection">Contact Us</a>
35            </li>
36        </ul>
37
38        <form class="form-inline my-2 my-lg-0">
39            <input class="form-control mr-sm-2" type="text"
                placeholder="Search">
40
41            <button class="btn btn-outline-success my-2
                my-sm-0" type="submit">Search</button>
42        </form>
43    </div>
```

You might be wondering why we left the unordered list and only removed its items. Leaving it forces the search input and **Search** button to remain anchored to the right. This section from the HEADER.php file will now look as follows:

```
23        <div class="collapse navbar-collapse" id="
          navbarTogglerDemo02">
24          <ul class="navbar-nav mr-auto mt-2 mt-md-0">
25
26          </ul>
27
28          <form class="form-inline my-2 my-lg-0">
29            <input class="form-control mr-sm-2" type="text"
                placeholder="Search">
30
31            <button class="btn btn-outline-success my-2
                my-sm-0" type="submit">Search</button>
32          </form>
33        </div>
```

Refactoring the index.js file

Just as we did with the index.css and index.php files, we will remove most of the code from the index.js file. Remove all code first function so the code looks as follows:

```
1 $( function( )
2 {
3
4 } );
```

We are now done, the website will look similar to the following screenshot:

 This refactored project can be found on the GitHub page https://github.com/PacktPublishing/Responsive-Web-Design-by-Example/tree/master

What will our blog home page look like?

Earlier in this chapter, we looked at many fantastic and innovative blog examples. Gawker is a nice clean blog that is used by many surfers around the world, but we will go with the layout presented on the TESCO blog as it has a variety of features. This will serve as an excellent foundation for more advanced blogs.

You probably noticed that all the blogs had a fixed width and weren't fluid, this is a very common layout for blogs. Though this isn't written in stone and a fluid layout can be used, tabloid style websites suit this fixed width layout, we will also be using this type of layout for our blog.

 Fluid spans the full width of the browser and fixed width does, but only to a set limit that varies from framework to framework. This limit is an industry standard.

Implementing the blog home page section

Our blog home page will consist of two main sections:

- Image slider/carousel to showcase blog posts
- All blog posts are presented using cards

Implementing the image slider

The first section will contain an image slider, also known as a carousel, which is intended to display highlighted posts/content.

Simple image slider

Firstly, we will create an image slider that automatically scrolls and has no buttons or captions.

Add the following code to the `index.php` file:

```php
1  <?php require_once( "SNIPPETS/HEADER.php" ); ?>
2
3  <div class="container">
4    <div class="row">
5      <div class="col-12">
6        <div class="carousel slide" data-ride="carousel">
7          <div class="carousel-inner" role="listbox">
8            <div class="carousel-item active">
9              <img class="d-block img-fluid" src="http://
                 res.cloudinary.com/dmliyxggm/image/upload/
                 v1511700177/large1_kfvfzm.jpg" alt="First
                 slide">
10           </div>
11
12           <div class="carousel-item">
13             <img class="d-block img-fluid" src="http://
                 res.cloudinary.com/dmliyxggm/image/upload/
                 v1511700177/large1_kfvfzm.jpg" alt="Second
                 slide">
14           </div>
15
16           <div class="carousel-item">
17             <img class="d-block img-fluid" src="http://
                 res.cloudinary.com/dmliyxggm/image/upload/
                 v1511700177/large1_kfvfzm.jpg" alt="Third
                 slide">
18           </div>
19         </div>
20       </div>
21     </div>
22   </div>
23 </div>
24
25 <?php require_once( "SNIPPETS/FOOTER.php" ); ?>
```

Let's run through the lines of code we just added:

- **Line 3** adds a fixed width container, nothing new here.
- **Line 4** adds a row, again nothing new here.
- **Line 5** adds a `div` that spans all 12 columns on all screen sizes.
- **Line 6** adds the carousels parent container with the functionality set to slide automatically.
- **Line 7** creates the inner section to store all the different slides.
- **Line 8** creates a carousel item/slide and is set to active so it is displayed first.
- **Line 9** creates an image to be displayed in the slide
- The remaining code simply repeats the first slide two more times without them being set to active. I have chosen to use the same image, but different images can easily be used.

The `src` tag can easily be changed to replace the image with a local one or one stored on a server/CDN.

The image used in the carousel is from `http://res.cloudinary.com/dmliyxggm/image/upload/v1511700177/large1_kfvfzm.jpg`

All this produces the following result:

On your screen you will see the carousel sliding between slides. But there is something wrong, I would recommend going to the original image as it looks like this:

The image in the carousel has been squashed, the severity of this will depend on the exact width of the browser. Try resizing the browser and see what happens, it definitely isn't what we would expect, yes the width should adjust, but the height should scale along with it hence maintaining the aspect ratio.

To do this is extremely simple, first add a class of `carouselImage` to each image inside of the carousel's slides like so:

```php
1  <?php require_once( "SNIPPETS/HEADER.php" ); ?>
2
3  <div class="container">
4    <div class="row">
5      <div class="col-12">
6        <div class="carousel slide" data-ride="carousel">
7          <div class="carousel-inner" role="listbox">
8            <div class="carousel-item active">
9              <img class="d-block img-fluid carouselImage"
                   src="http://res.cloudinary.    n/dmliyxggm/image
                   /upload/v1511700177/larg     vfzm.jpg" alt="
                   First slide">
10           </div>
11
12           <div class="carousel-item">
13             <img class="d                      carouselImage
                   src="http://res.cloudinar .com/dmliyxggm/image
                   /upload/v1511700177/large1_kfvfzm.jpg" alt="
                   Second slide">
14           </div>
15
16           <div class="carousel-item">
17             <img class="d-block img-fluid carouselImage
                   src="http://res.cloudinary.com/dmliyxggm/image
                   /upload/v1511700177/large1_kfvfzm.jpg" alt="
                   Third slide">
18           </div>
19         </div>
20       </div>
21     </div>
22   </div>
23 </div>
24
25 <?php require_once( "SNIPPETS/FOOTER.php" ); ?>
```

Now add the following styling code to the `index.css` file:

```css
6  .carouselImage
7  {
8      width: 100%;
9      height: 100%;
10 }
```

This will now ensure that the image covers 100% of the rows width and dynamically adjusts the height to maintain the original aspect ratio. The great thing about this implementation is it allows images of any ratio, thus reducing more potential changes for you as the developer. The website's carousel now looks as follows:

Adding back and forward buttons to the slider

At the moment our carousel has three slides, but imagine if it had 10 and you missed a particular slide with the information you wanted. It wouldn't be a very good user experience if you had to wait for it to come back for you to just miss it again. Luckily we can alleviate this nuisance with buttons that provide linear navigation.

First we need to add an `id` to the carousel container as this will be used to link the backward and forward buttons. Simply add an `id` of `AwesomeCarousel` like so:

```
6    <div id="AwesomeCarousel" class="carousel slide"
     data-ride="carousel">
7        <div class="carousel-inner" role="listbox">
8            <div class="carousel-item active">
9                <img class="d-block img-fluid carouselImage"
                 src="http://res.cloudinary.com/dmliyxggm/image
                 /upload/v1511700177/large1_kfvfzm.jpg" alt="
                 First slide">
10           </div>
11
12           <div class="carousel-item">
13               <img class="d-block img-fluid carouselImage"
                 src="http://res.cloudinary.com/dmliyxggm/image
                 /upload/v1511700177/large1_kfvfzm.jpg" alt="
                 Second slide">
14           </div>
15
16           <div class="carousel-item">
17               <img class="d-block img-fluid carouselImage"
                 src="http://res.cloudinary.com/dmliyxggm/image
                 /upload/v1511700177/large1_kfvfzm.jpg" alt="
                 Third slide">
18           </div>
19       </div>
20   </div>
```

Now add the following code below the inner carousel container:

```
6      <div id="AwesomeCarousel" class="carousel slide"
       data-ride="carousel">
7        <div class="carousel-inner" role="listbox">
8          <div class="carousel-item active">
9            <img class="d-block img-fluid carouselImage"
             src="http://res.cloudinary.com/dmliyxggm/image
             /upload/v1511700177/large1_kfvfzm.jpg" alt="
             First slide">
10         </div>
11
12         <div class="carousel-item">
13           <img class="d-block img-fluid carouselImage"
             src="http://res.cloudinary.com/dmliyxggm/image
             /upload/v1511700177/large1_kfvfzm.jpg" alt="
             Second slide">
14         </div>
15
16         <div class="carousel-item">
17           <img class="d-block img-fluid carouselImage"
             src="http://res.cloudinary.com/dmliyxggm/image
             /upload/v1511700177/large1_kfvfzm.jpg" alt="
             ird slide">
18         </di
19       </div>
20
21       <a class="carousel-control-prev" href="
         #AwesomeCarousel" role="button" data-slide="prev">
22         <span class="carousel-control-prev-icon"
           aria-hidden="true"></span>
23         <span class="sr-only">Previous</span>
24       </a>
25
26       <a class="carousel-control-next" href="
         #AwesomeCarousel" role="button" data-slide="next">
27         <span class="carousel-control-next-icon"
           aria-hidden="true"></span>
28         <span class="sr-only">Next</span>
29       </a>
30     </div>
```

Let's go through the code we added line by line:

- **Line 21** adds the back button container, which also links to the carousel using the ID we added
- **Line 22** adds the back icon
- **Line 23** is intended for screen readers
- **Line 26** adds the forward button container, which also links to the carousel using the ID we added
- **Line 27** adds the forward icon
- **Line 28** is intended for screen readers

This produces the following navigation system within the carousel:

Bootstrap goes next level genius with the carousel buttons as you don't need to specifically click on the button, but merely that edge of the carousel to navigate. Give it a go and see what you think.

Carousel indicators

We have an awesome fully functional carousel, but what if the user wants to go to a specific slide, do they keep clicking until they get there? Again this poor user experience will deter users from using our website.

This is where indicators come to the rescue. They are essentially buttons to easily navigate directly to a specific slide. Add the following code above the inner carousel `div`:

```
6    <div id="AwesomeCarousel" class="carousel slide"
     data-ride="carousel">
7      <ol class="carousel-indicators">
8        <li data-target="#AwesomeCarousel" data-slide-to
         ="0" class="active"></li>
9        <li data-target="#AwesomeCarousel" data-slide-to
         ="1"></li>
10       <li data-target="#AwesomeCarousel" data-slide-to
         ="2"></li>
11     </ol>
12
13     <div class="carousel-i      " role="listbox">
14       <div class="car      em active">
15         <img class="d-b     img-fluid carouselImage"
           src="http://r    .c oudinary.com/dmliyxggm/image
           /upload/v15   700177/large1_kfvfzm.jpg" alt="
           First sli   ">
16       </div>
17
18       <div  lass="carousel-item">
19         mg class="d-block img-fluid carouselImage"
           rc="http://res.cloudinary.com/dmliyxggm/image
           /upload/v1511700177/large1_kfvfzm.jpg" alt="
           Second slide">
20       </div>
21
22       <div class="carousel-item">
23         <img class="d-block img-fluid carouselImage"
           src="http://res.cloudinary.com/dmliyxggm/image
           /upload/v1511700177/large1_kfvfzm.jpg" alt="
           Third slide">
24       </div>
25     </div>
```

Let's go over the new code line by line:

- **Line 7** adds a list of indicators, which will form the basis of our navigation
- **Line 8** adds the first indicator and links it to the first slide and sets it to active
- **Line 9** adds the second indicator and links it to the first slide and sets it to active
- **Line 10** adds the third indicator and links it to the first slide and sets it to active

The active class should match the slide number it is applied to so it loads correctly.

As you are most likely aware, many aspects of computing start at 0 and not 1, this is also the case for the indicators.

For every slide added/removed make sure the same changes are made to the indicators.

All of this produces the following result:

We now have some really awesome indicators at the bottom for improved navigation.

Captioning our carousel

This is the final part of our carousel, adding some captions. It is very common for carousel slides to have individual text, you could add it to the image, but this text usually is slide-specific and can easily change. Using a normal image without the captioned text allows it to be reused in other areas thus reducing time creating/sourcing new images.

Captions are very easy to add, simply update any carousel item with the following code to add a caption header and body:

```
14    <div class="carousel-item active">
15        <img class="d-block img-fluid carouselImage"
          src="http://res.cloudinary.com/dmliyxggm/image
          /upload/v1511700177/large1_kfvfzm.jpg" alt="
          First slide">
16
17        <div class="carousel-caption d-none d-md-block
          ">
18            <h3>Slide 1</h3>
19            <p>Extremely important, please read!!!</p>
20        </div>
21    </div>
```

Let's go over the new code line by line:

- **Line 17** adds a `div` to store all the caption data using bootstrap classes. `D-md-block` is an important class as it sets the caption block to only appear on screen sizes that are medium or larger. This can be easily changed to show the caption on different screen sizes using the information covered in *Chapter 2, What Is Bootstrap, Why Do We Use It?*.
- **Line 18** adds a header for the slide's caption.
- **Line 19** adds the captions main body.

I have only added a caption to the first slide, but you can easily add it to any of the slides. I would recommend doing this as an extra task.

This will produce the following caption on the first slide on screen sizes that are medium or larger:

The carousel is now complete, but Bootstrap as usual is awesome and provides a plethora of functionality to manipulate the carousel using JavaScript. To see more information regarding this, check out the following link `https://v4-alpha.getbootstrap.com/components/carousel/`

 The slides can easily be enclosed within `<a href>` tags to allow navigation to a blog post or an external website.

Implementing the blog posts

Now we will implement the blog posts on the home page, these will not be the full post, but a snippet to get the user's appetite wet and entice them to click on it.

Let's take a look at the blog post preview from the TESCO blog:

The preceding post consists of the following:

- A thumbnail image
- Category
- Title
- Brief description
- Share button, which when clicked shows the following buttons:

TESCO's blog uses tiles to display the posts, Bootstrap has a really cool feature called **cards** that provide a very similar look and feel.

For more information about the card component in Bootstrap check out the following link:

```
https://v4-alpha.getbootstrap.com/components/card/
```

Adding cards

Now we all add some cards to our home page, simply add the following code after the row that contained the carousel:

```
37      <a class="carousel-control-next" href="
        #AwesomeCarousel" role="button" data-slide="next">
38        <span class="carousel-control-next-icon"
        aria-hidden="true"></span>
39        <span class="sr-only">Next</span>
40      </a>
41    </div>
42  </div>
43 </div>
44
45 <div class="row">
46   <div class="col-lg-4 col-md-6">
47     <div class="card">
48       <a href="post.php"><img class="card-img-top
       cardImage" src=" http://res.cloudinary.com/
       dmliyxggm/image/upload/v1511702046/
       poster_ysydov.jpg" alt="Card image cap"></a>
49
50       <div class="card-block">
51         <a href="post.php"><h4 class="card-title">
       Trekking</h4></a>
52
53         <p class="card-text">Lorem ipsum dolor sit amet
       </p>
54       </div>
55     </div>
56   </div>
57 </div>
58 </div>
59
60 <?php require_once( "SNIPPETS/FOOTER.php" ); ?>
```

Let's go over the code line by line:

- **Line 1** adds a row like we have already done a million times already.
- **Line 2** adds a `div` that will store a single card. The classes provide the following layout:
  - Large screen sizes will display three cards on the same row
  - Medium screens will display two cards on the same row
  - Small and extra small screen sizes will display a single card on each row

  Again row refers to the literal row and not the row class.

- **Line 3** adds a Bootstrap card.
- **Line 4** creates an image enclosed in a link to navigate to the post page which will be created and implemented in the next chapter. Clicking on it as of now will produce an error, don't worry this will be fixed in the next chapter.
- **Line 6** adds a section that will contain the text for the card.
- **Line 7** adds a title to the card that is also linked to the post page.
- **Line 9** adds a paragraph to entice the viewer and provide some information regarding the post.

I have only added one post in the preceding code. But to add more merely duplicate the following code and make any of the following relevant changes:

- Image
- Title
- Description text
- Link, maybe you want it to link to another website

```html
<div class="col-lg-4 col-md-6">
  <div class="card">
    <a href="post.php"><img class="card-img-top
    cardImage" src=" http://res.cloudinary.com/
    dmliyxggm/image/upload/v1511702046/
    poster_ysydov.jpg" alt="Card image cap"></a>

    <div class="card-block">
      <a href="post.php"><h4 class="card-title">
      Trekking</h4></a>

      <p class="card-text">Lorem ipsum dolor sit amet
      </p>
    </div>
  </div>
</div>
```

This all produces the following result:

As you can see, it's all a bit of a mess and the image size isn't constrained to the card. Fortunately, to do this only requires a single line of CSS code. First add a class of `cardImage` to the card images like so:

```
<div class="col-lg-4 col-md-6">
  <div class="card">
    <a href="post.php"><img class="card-img-top
    cardImage  src=" http://res.cloudinary.com/
    dmliyx...m/image/upload/v1511702046/
    poster_...ov.jpg" alt="Card image cap"></a>

    <div class="card-block">
      <a href="post.php"><h4 class="card-title">
      Trekking</h4></a>

      <p class="card-text">Lorem ipsum dolor sit amet
      </p>
    </div>
  </div>
</div>
```

Add the following style code to the `index.css` file:

```
12 .cardImage
13 {
14      width: 100%;
15 }
```

This will now produce the following more elegant card layout:

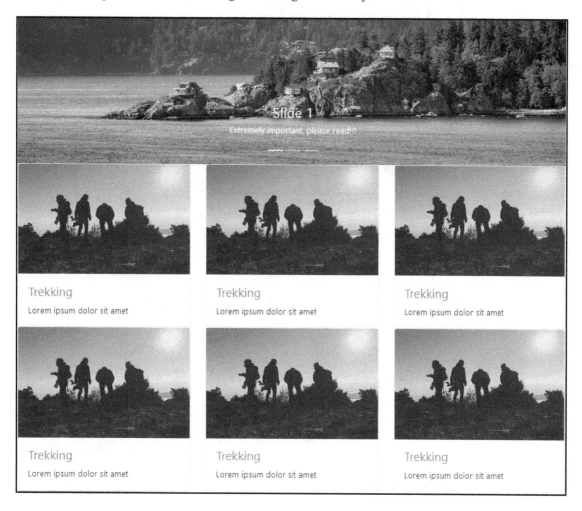

But there are still two small problems. The first is that there is no gap at the bottom of each card, the second there is no gap between the carousel and the cards. Fortunately for us this is extremely easy to fix, add a class of `cardContainer` to the following `div`:

```
<div class="col-lg-4 col-md-6 cardContainer">
  <div class="card">
    <a href="post.php"><img class=    rd-img-top
    cardImage" src=" http://res.    o  inary.com/
    dmliyxggm/image/upload/v151  02046/
    poster_ysydov.jpg" alt="C  d image cap"></a>

    <div class="card-block ">
      <a href="post.php"><h4 class="card-title">
      Trekking</h4></a>

      <p class="card-text">Lorem ipsum dolor sit amet
      </p>
    </div>
  </div>
</div>
```

Add the following style code to the `index.css` file:

```
17 .cardContainer
18 {
19     margin-top: 10px;
20 }
```

This all produces the following amazing card layout:

And we are done, the card system and the carousel is now fully implemented and provides our blog with an amazing responsive blog home page. As usual I recommend resizing the browser to see how it responsively reacts to our implementation.

Summary

In this chapter, we implemented the blog's home page, which will serve as a great foundation. The card system we used is very common on a wide range of social networks.

In the next chapter, we will embark on the journey to create a blog post page to display more detail about a blog post.

8
Creating the Blog Posts Page

This chapter will finish our blog. We will create the post page, which will display a blog post in full detail instead of a preview. We will cover creating a new page using our Reusable Project Template.

In this chapter, we will cover the following topics:

- Bootstrap/HTML headers
- Bootstrap showcase images
- HTML paragraphs
- Media embedding
- Debugging and testing responsive design

Blog post page examples

Before we take a look at some blog post examples, let's think about some of the most important things a blog post page needs:

- Title
- Something to entice the reader, usually an image
- A quick overview of the article

Now, let's go through some examples of blog post pages for further enlightenment, which will aid in developing our very own. We will look at the same websites that we covered in the preceding chapter.

TechCrunch

TechCrunch has a lot going on outside of the main post, from popular posts to newsletters and other latest news.

Its website link is `https://techcrunch.com/2017/07/16/lenovo-teases-augmented-reality-headset-for-new-star-wars-experience/`

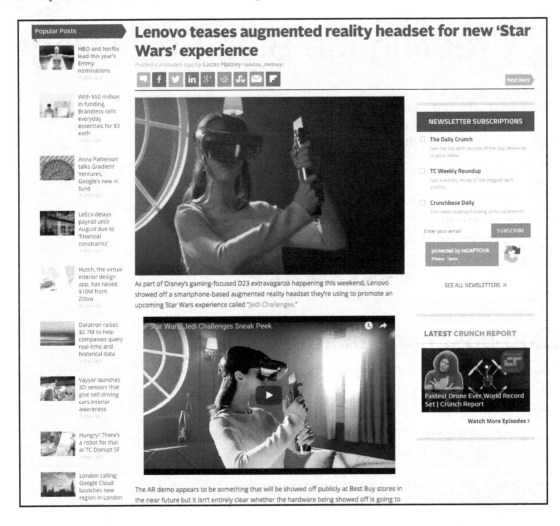

Any blog post from TechCrunch is good to view; note that it doesn't have to be the same one as mentioned here.

Gawker

Gawker is simple, but elegantly effective. The blog content is displayed in a linear fashion using simple HTML elements.

Its website link is `http://gawker.com/letters-from-our-exes-1785587207`

Microsoft News

Microsoft News has nice background animations and images, and is similar in layout to Gawker, but more flashy.

Its website link is `https://news.microsoft.com/stories/block-by-block/`

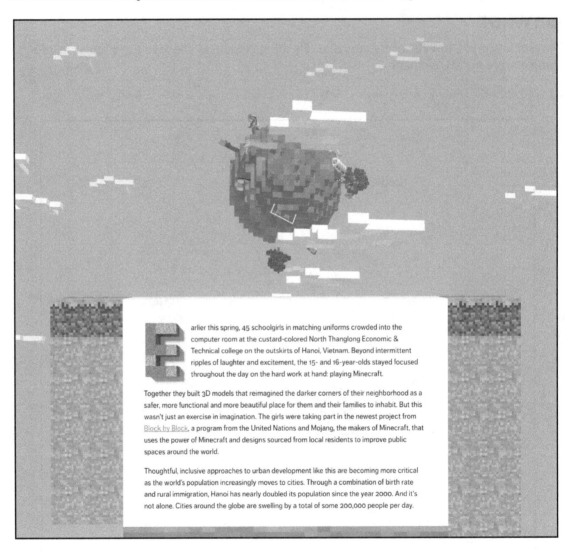

arlier this spring, 45 schoolgirls in matching uniforms crowded into the computer room at the custard-colored North Thanglong Economic & Technical college on the outskirts of Hanoi, Vietnam. Beyond intermittent ripples of laughter and excitement, the 15- and 16-year-olds stayed focused throughout the day on the hard work at hand: playing Minecraft.

Together they built 3D models that reimagined the darker corners of their neighborhood as a safer, more functional and more beautiful place for them and their families to inhabit. But this wasn't just an exercise in imagination. The girls were taking part in the newest project from Block by Block, a program from the United Nations and Mojang, the makers of Minecraft, that uses the power of Minecraft and designs sourced from local residents to improve public spaces around the world.

Thoughtful, inclusive approaches to urban development like this are becoming more critical as the world's population increasingly moves to cities. Through a combination of birth rate and rural immigration, Hanoi has nearly doubled its population since the year 2000. And it's not alone. Cities around the globe are swelling by a total of some 200,000 people per day.

Johnny Cupcakes

Johnny Cupcakes is similar to Gawker and Microsoft, but it uses very big pictures to illustrate the purpose of the article.

Its website link is `http://kitchen.johnnycupcakes.com/blog/2016/08/johnny-cupcakes-x-san-francisco/`

Tesco Living

Tesco's page is clean; however, it still incorporates some cool features such as the popular and recommended sections.

Its website link is https://www.tesco.com/

What will our blog post page consist of?

You're probably wondering what our page will look like. Drum roll, we will base it on the Tesco page.

Let's take a look at what the page consists of. There are two main sections:

- Post content
- Extra navigation to popular and recommended articles

This is the first instance where we will essentially have a sidebar. Take a look at the Tesco page and see how it looks on different devices. As you can probably tell, when the width is too small the sidebar becomes a new section below it, which can be achieved using the grid skills we have already covered multiple times in previous chapters.

What does the post content consist of?

We now know the overall content structure of the post page, but what will the post content actually contain? If you take a look at the Tesco page, you will note the following items/sections:

- Title
- Social share buttons
- Post banner image
- Small paragraph to grab the viewer's attention
- Main body which consists of text and images
- More useful links
- Social share button (same as the ones at the top of the article)

We will follow the exact same layout with the exclusion of the social buttons. The reason for this is simple, we have completed a single project and have almost completed our second, the social buttons implementation will be left as an extra task for you.

What does the popular and recommended sidebar consists of?

The popular and recommended sections are both structured the same way; they both consist of the following items:

- Title
- Underline to separate the title and content
- Section to group each item's content:
    - Thumbnail image
    - Item title

We are now ready to start coding our blog post page.

Implementing the blog post page

Before we can even create the main content body and sidebar, we will first need a new file. If you recall, in the previous chapter, we linked all of the blog post previews to a nonexistent `post.php` page. Now, we will finally create that page; simply create a new file in the root directory alongside `index.php` called `post.php`. The project structure will now be as follows:

- CSS
- Images
- index.php
- JS
- post.php
- SNIPPETS

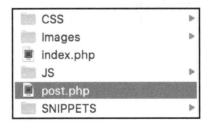

Now the directory structure is in-line with the preceding screenshot, we can truly use the Reusable Project Template we set up in `Chapter 3`. Without the Reusable Project Template, we would have had to duplicate all the header and footer code in the `post.php` file as well. Luckily for us, all that is required are the two require lines to retrieve the header and footer code. Add the following code to your `post.php` file:

```
1 <?php require_once( "SNIPPETS/HEADER.php" ); ?>
2
3
4 <?php require_once( "SNIPPETS/FOOTER.php" ); ?>
```

This produces the following unexciting result:

Don't worry! We will soon be adding the page's main content and sections.

Implementing the post's main content

We know what the main content section will contain—if you need a quick refresher, don't worry, go back to the start of this chapter and take a look at the examples we covered; I'll be waiting right here for you.

Adding the blog post title and banner image

Add the following code to your `post.php` file:

```
1  <?php require_once( "SNIPPETS/HEADER.php" ); ?>
2
3  <div class="container">
4    <div class="row">
5      <div class="col-lg-9">
6        <h1>Trekking</h1>
7
8        <img src="http://res.cloudinary.com/dmliyxggm/image/
         upload/v1511702046/poster_ysydov.jpg" />
9      </div>
10   </div>
11 </div>
12
13 <?php require_once( "SNIPPETS/FOOTER.php" ); ?>
```

Let's go over the new code line by line:

- **Line 1** adds a container to store all of our page's content
- **Line 2** creates a row to store the main section
- **Line 3** creates a `div`, which will span 9 columns on bigger screens; on small screens, it will span 12 columns
- **Line 4** adds a simple title
- **Line 6** creates a big image to be used as the post's banner

The code we just added produces the following result:

Again, as we did in the preceding section, we will need to set the image's width to always be 100%. Add an `id` of `PostImageBanner` to the image, like so:

```
1  <?php require_once( "SNIPPETS/HEADER.php" ); ?>
2
3  <div class="container">
4    <div class="row">
5      <div class="col-lg-9">
6        <h1>Trekking</h1>
7
8        <img id="PostImageBanner" src="http://
           res.cloudinary.com/dmliyx   m/image/upload/v1511702046
           /poster_ysydov.jpg" />
9      </div>
10   </div>
11 </div>
12
13 <?php require_once( "SNIPPETS/FOOTER.php" ); ?>
```

Now, add the code to achieve this to the `index.css` file:

```
22 #PostImageBanner
23 {
24     width: 100%;
25 }
```

 The reason an `id` was used is that there will only be a single image banner for each post. There may be more than one image, but they will have a different style.

This produces the following result:

It may not look very different. However, you can just resize the browser with and without the new code to truly see the benefit of this minimal but crucial CSS implementation.

Adding the snapshot paragraph

Now, let's implement a small snippet of text that is designed to draw the viewer's attention and keep them on the page and reading. It is very common for this to be a question. Add the following code just after the image created in the preceding section:

```php
1  <?php require_once( "SNIPPETS/HEADER.php" ); ?>
2
3  <div class="container">
4    <div class="row">
5      <div class="col-lg-9">
6        <h1>Trekking</h1>
7
8        <img id="PostImageBanner" src="http://
           res.cloudinary.com/dmliyxggm/image/upload/v1511702046
           /poster_ysydov.jpg" />
9
10       <h3>Lorem ipsum dolor sit amet, consectetur
           adipiscing elit, sed do eiusmod tempor incididunt ut
           labore et dolore magna aliqua. Ut enim ad minim
           veniam, quis nostrud exercitation ullamco laboris
           nisi ut aliquip ex ea commodo consequat.</h3>
11     </div>
12   </div>
13 </div>
14
15 <?php require_once( "SNIPPETS/FOOTER.php" ); ?>
```

 We have created a simple header; you can add some color to it and use a different font, but this is a very simple element of the main content. Now, let's see what this looks like:

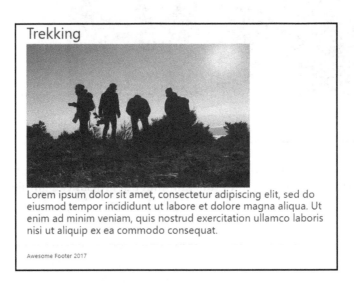

Trekking

Lorem ipsum dolor sit amet, consectetur adipiscing elit, sed do eiusmod tempor incididunt ut labore et dolore magna aliqua. Ut enim ad minim veniam, quis nostrud exercitation ullamco laboris nisi ut aliquip ex ea commodo consequat.

Awesome Footer 2017

As per usual, it needs some modifications; there needs to be a bigger gap between the image and text to make it look more professional. We will add a margin to the bottom of the image. Luckily, we already have a way of accessing the image through its id, which was added earlier in this chapter. Now, add the following styling in the index.css file:

```
22 #PostImageBanner
23 {
24     width: 100%;
25     margin-bottom: 35px;
26 }
```

We added a margin at the bottom of the image of 35 pixels; this value can be tweaked to suit your needs. This now moves the text down, as can be seen here:

Trekking

Lorem ipsum dolor sit amet, consectetur adipiscing elit, sed do eiusmod tempor incididunt ut labore et dolore magna aliqua. Ut enim ad minim veniam, quis nostrud exercitation ullamco laboris nisi ut aliquip ex ea commodo consequat.

Awesome Footer 2017

Adding the body

Now, we will add the main article that viewers have come to read. This can consist of a wide variety of elements, such as the following:

- Text
- Images
- Links
- Videos
- Forms

Essentially, they will be anything that can be added to a website and can be placed in the main article section. We will keep it simple and add some text along with an image, similar to the Tesco blog article we discussed earlier in this chapter. Add the following code below the snapshot paragraph:

```
3  <div class="container">
4    <div class="row">
5      <div class="col-lg-9">
6        <h1>Trekking</h1>
7
8        <img id="PostImageBanner" src="http://
         res.cloudinary.com/dmliyxggm/image/upload/v1511702046
         /poster_ysydov.jpg" />
9
10       <h3>Lorem ipsum dolor sit amet, consectetur
         adipiscing elit, sed do eiusmod tempor incididunt ut
         labore et dolore magna aliqua. Ut enim ad minim
         veniam, quis nostrud exercitation ullamco laboris
         nisi ut aliquip ex ea commodo consequat.</h3>
11
12       <h6>Sub Heading</h6>
13
14       <p>Lorem ipsum dolor sit amet, consectetur
         adipiscing elit, sed do eiusmod tempor incididunt ut
         labore et dolore magna aliqua. Ut enim ad minim
         veniam, quis nostrud exercitation ullamco laboris
         nisi ut aliquip ex ea commodo consequat. Duis aute
         irure dolor in reprehenderit in voluptate velit esse
         cillum dolore eu fugiat nulla pariatur. Excepteur
         sint occaecat cupidatat non proident, sunt in culpa
         qui officia deserunt mollit anim id est laborum.</p>
15
16       <img src="http://res.cloudinary.com/dmliyxggm/image/
         upload/v1511708668/
         subheading_cxcp24.png?w=760&h=427&l=50&t=40" />
17     </div>
18   </div>
19 </div>
```

It's very simple; we added a subheading and a paragraph along with an image. Naturally, these will reflect the subject of the article, so feel free to change them. Let's take a look at the result:

There are two problems that need to be addressed, which are as follows:

- The subheading is directly below the snapshot paragraph. There should be a larger gap similar to the poster image and the snapshot paragraph.
- The image is too big and needs to be constrained.

First, let's deal with the gap issue. Add an `id` of `PostSnapshot` to the snapshot paragraph:

```
6    <h1>Trekking</h1>
7
8    <img id="PostImageBanner" src="http://
     res.cloudinary.com/dmlivxgqp/image/upload/v1511702046
     /poster_ysydov.jpg" />
9
10   <h3 id="PostSnapshot">Lorem ipsum dolor sit amet,
     consectetur adipiscing elit, sed do eiusmod tempor
     incididunt ut labore et dolore magna aliqua. Ut enim
     ad minim veniam, quis nostrud exercitation ullamco
     laboris nisi ut aliquip ex ea commodo consequat.</h3>
```

We will now add a margin to the bottom of the snapshot paragraph. We will make it the same as the margin below the poster image for consistency. However, these values can be changed and can also be different, if you so desire:

```
28 #PostSnapshot
29 {
30      margin-bottom: 35px;
31 }
```

This will move the main article down, as can be witnessed here:

One problem fixed, one more to go. Now, let's constrain the image so that it doesn't overflow. It may not look like it's overflowing at the moment, but once we add the sidebar, it will; so, let's fix this problem now. First, add a `postArticleImage` class to the image:

```
12      <h6>Sub Heading</h6>
13
14      <p>Lorem ipsum dolor sit amet, consectetur
        adipiscing elit, sed do eiusmod tempor incididunt ut
        labore et dolore magna aliqua. Ut enim ad minim
        veniam, quis nostrud exercitation ullamco laboris
        nisi ut aliquip ex ea commodo consequat. Duis aute
        irure dolor in reprehenderit in voluptate velit esse
        cillum dolore eu fugiat nulla pariatur. Excepteur
        sint occaecat cupidatat non proident, sunt in culpa
        qui officia deserunt mollit anim id est laborum.</p>
15
16      <img class="postArticleImage" src="http://
        res.cloudinary.com/dmliyxggm/image/upload/v1511708668
        /subheading_cxcp24.png?w=760&h=427&l=50&t=40" />
```

We use a class as this will allow the styling that will follow to be easily applied to other images within the main article, as it is a common practice to have multiple images. Now, add the following styling code to the `index.css` file:

```
33 .postArticleImage
34 {
35      width: 75%;
36 }
```

I have chosen a width of 75% of the parent container to not overpower the importance of the poster image at the top. This now produces the following result:

This has fixed the overflow problem but created another one. The image isn't centered; while this isn't necessary, it does improve the overall layout. To do this, all we have to do is add a margin to the left of the image, as follows:

```
33 .postArticleImage
34 {
35     width: 75%;
36     margin-left: 12.5%;
37 }
```

You're probably thinking where did the `12.5%` value come from? It's actually extremely simple, but genius. We have an image that has a width of 75% of its parent container; this leaves us with 25% in the container. We don't want to move it 25%, as this will align the image to the right, so we want half of the remaining space, which is 12.5%. An alternative could be to encapsulate the image within a `div` and center it using the text center property.

If the width of the image is changed, then the margin will also need to be updated using the process discussed above.

This produces the following result:

Now, let's move on to the final part of this main body section.

More useful links

We are almost done. It is extremely common for blog posts to have some useful links for the viewer; these can be internal or external links. There is nothing more to it than that; add the following code to our website:

```
16      <img class="postArticleImage" src="http://
        res.cloudinary.com/dmliyxggm/image/upload/v1511708668
        /subheading_cxcp24.png?w=760&h=427&l=50&t=40" />
17
18      <h4>More Useful Links</h4>
19
20      <ul>
21        <li><a href="http://www.sonarlearning.co.uk">Sonar
          Learning</a></li>
22
23        <li><a href="http://www.sonarsystems.co.uk">Sonar
          Systems</a></li>
24      </ul>
25    </div>
```

Feel free to change the links to whatever you want and add more as you see fit. This produces the following result:

That dreaded problem is back; there needs to be more of a gap between the image and the heading. I'm sure that you're already aware of how to do this, but let's quickly recap. Add an id of PostLinksHeader, like so:

```
<h4 id="PostLinksHeader">More Useful Links</h4>

<ul>
  <li><a href="http://www.sonarlearning.co.uk">Sonar
  Learning</a></li>

  <li><a href="http://www.sonarsystems.co.uk">Sonar
  Systems</a></li>
</ul>
```

Now, add the following styling to the index.css file:

```
39 #PostLinksHeader
40 {
41      margin-top: 35px;
42 }
```

We added a margin to the top to provide a gap between the image and the useful links section. Let's see our beauty:

We are now done with the main section on this page; let's move on to the sidebar.

Implementing the sidebar

We are now at the final stage of this chapter, where we implement a sidebar with call links to other great articles. As you may remember from earlier in this chapter , we added a `div`, which spanned only nine columns on larger screens, and the remaining three are for the sidebar. To access them, add the following code below the `div` that contains all the main content:

```
20      <ul>
21          <li><a href="http://www.sonarlearning.co.uk">Sonar
            Learning</a></li>
22
23          <li><a href="http://www.sonarsystems.co.uk">Sonar
            Systems</a></li>
24      </ul>
25      </div>
26
27      <div class="col-lg-3">
28          <h2>Popular</h2>
29
30          <hr />
31      </div>
32  </div>
33  </div>
34
35  <?php require_once( "SNIPPETS/FOOTER.php" ); ?>
```

The code we added simply creates a `div` to contain the sidebar and adds a section header along with a horizontal rule. This will produce the following result:

This is a good start, but the horizontal line is barely visible; I wouldn't blame you if you can't see it—it is, after all, that faint. We will override the border properties to change the size and color. First, add a class of `postSidebarLine` to the horizontal rule tag:

```
27      <div class="col-lg-3">
28          <h2>Popular</h2>
29
30          <hr class="
            postSidebarLine" />
31      </div>
```

Now, add the following code to the `index.css` file to override the default properties of the horizontal rule tag:

```
44 .postSidebarLine
45 {
46     border-top: 7px solid
            #00549E;
47 }
```

We simply changed the height of the border to 7px and changed the color to the one used on the Tesco blog; feel free to change these properties to suit your vision. This all produces the following result:

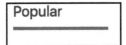

A class was used to allow multiple sections within the sidebar to adopt the same style using a single code base; as an extra task, add extra sections as seen in the Tesco blog website.

Now, it is time to add the popular links along with a thumbnail to attract the viewer. Add the following code below the horizontal tag:

```
27     <div class="col-lg-3">
28       <h2>Popular</h2>
29
30       <hr class="postSidebarLine" />
31
32       <div class="col-lg-12 col-md-6">
33         <img src="Images/Article Thumbnail.jpg" />
34
35         <span>Lorem ipsum </span>
36       </div>
37     </div>
```

We applied another column system to the containing `div`, as the sidebar will actually appear below the main content on smaller screens, which will provide more room horizontally so that we can have more than one image next to each other on medium screen sizes. I have added a file locally, but as usual it could be stored online via a CDN. This will produce the following result:

As you can see, this isn't what we want at all; the image is having the same problem in that it is overflowing. This can be fixed very easily; first, add a class of `postPopularImage` to the image:

```
27    <div class="col-lg-3">
28      <h2>Popular</h2>
29
30      <hr class="postSidebarLine" />
31
32      <div class="col-lg-12 col-md-6">
33        <img class="postPopularImage" src="Images/
          Article Thumbnail.jpg" />
34
35        <span>Lorem ipsum </span>
36      </div>
37    </div>
```

Now, add the following code to the `index.css` file to restrict the size of the image:

```
49 .postPopularImage
50 {
51      width: 75px;
52 }
```

I have set the width to 75px, which also locks the height as well, but you can make it smaller or bigger as you see fit. This now looks a lot better, as can be seen in the following screenshot:

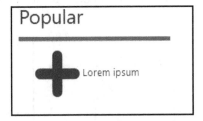

We are almost done; by default, Bootstrap applies padding to a lot of its classes, including the column classes, that pushes the image to the right. Let's remove this padding which will provide more room for the content. Add a class of postPopularContainer to the div containing the popular content, like so:

```
27    <div class="col-lg-3">
28        <h2>Popular</h2>
29
30        <hr class="postSidebarLine" />
31
32        <div class="col-lg-12 col-md-6 postPopularContainer">
33            <img class="postPopularImage" src="Images/Article
              Thumbnail.jpg" />
34
35            <span>Lorem ipsum </span>
36        </div>
37    </div>
```

Now, add the following code to the index.css file to remove the padding from the left and right:

```
54 .postPopularContainer
55 {
56      padding-left: 0;
57      padding-right: 0;
58 }
```

As you can see, the padding has been removed:

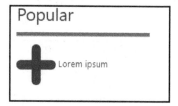

To add more articles in the sidebar, simply duplicate the following code and make the appropriate changes:

```
27    <div class="col-lg-3">
28      <h2>Popular</h2>
29
30      <hr class="postSidebarLine" />
31
32      <div class="col-lg-12 col-md-6 postPopularContainer">
33        <img class="postPopularImage" src="Images/Article
          Thumbnail.jpg" />
34
35        <span>Lorem ipsum </span>
36      </div>
37    </div>
```

This is what it will look like with multiple article previews:

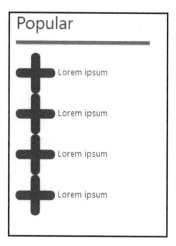

It's lucky we checked this out, as there is no gap below each preview. Fortunately for us, we just added a margin to the bottom of each `div` using the class of `postPopularContainer` that we have already implemented:

```
54 .postPopularContainer
55 {
56     padding-left: 0;
57     padding-right: 0;
58     margin-bottom: 10px;
59 }
```

Now, there is a gap below each article preview, as follows:

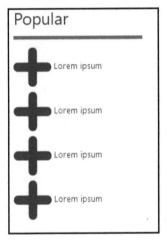

Let's test what it looks like on a medium screen where the sidebar is below the main content:

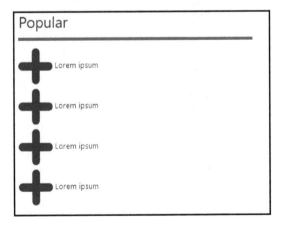

I don't know about you, but this doesn't look the way it should; there should be two previews next to each other on each row. Luckily, this can easily be fixed by enclosing all the previews within a `div` that has a class of `row`. I'm sure you're very familiar with how to do this by now. Making this change will produce the following result:

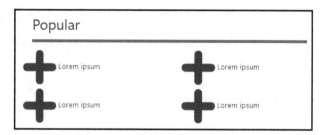

Okay, the previews are properly using the Bootstrap column classes that they have, but their content is slightly overflowing; this is due to the padding we removed. Remove the two lines that we added in the `index.css` file to remove the padding from the left and right. This will now produce the following result:

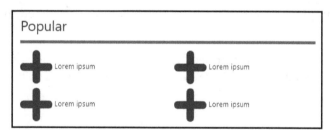

Excellent! We are now all done. You might be wondering why I went through all the hassle of not adding the row `div` and padding removal code—this was to demonstrate one of the common pitfalls and how to resolve it.

Further extending the blog

If you take a look at the examples at the beginning of this chapter, you will note that they have other content/features that we didn't cover.

It would be great if you could tackle some of these extra tasks for this project:

- Check out responsive media (video) at `https://v4-alpha.getbootstrap.com/utilities/responsive-helpers/`
- Animations using jQuery
- Check out social buttons at `http://www.addthis.com/`

Take a look, think of your own ideas, and then implement them to see how you can further extend the blog.

Summary

In this chapter, we implemented the blog post page, and we completed the second project in this book with that.

The next chapter will start the third project, which is a social network, and it will cover adding a really cool sidebar, even better than the one implemented in this chapter.

9
Adding a Sidebar to the Social Network

This chapter will help you start the social network using the preceding code base and add a sidebar for navigation. We will be incorporating many responsive features and philosophies when creating the sidebar; it will be significantly more advanced than the sidebar in the blog. We will do the sidebar as our first task, as it is more complex than the one added in the preceding chapter.

The topics covered in this chapter are as follows:

- Icons
- Bootstrap images
- Bootstrap cards/tiles
- HTML links
- Collapsible sidebar
- Debugging and testing Responsive Design

Social network sidebar examples

Let's go through some examples of sidebars used in social networks. There are an increasing number of social networks to choose and get inspiration from, and I'm sure that you have your own favorites; however, I would always recommend that you check all of them out first.

Facebook

Facebook is the most successful social network in human history, and, most likely, every reader at some point has had a Facebook account; it is definitely one to take inspiration from. Facebook's sidebar isn't collapsible and modern as some of the other examples that we will look at; it's website link is `https://www.facebook.com/`

Google+

Google+ may not be the first social network you visit, but with more than 100 million active users and a consistently modern design, it deserves a place on our list. This sidebar is collapsible unlike Facebook's; it's website link is `https://plus.google.com/`

YouTube

YouTube's design has similarities to Google+ for obvious reasons, but it is used to display different information; again, it can be hidden using the burger button located at the top left of the page; it's website link is `https://www.youtube.com/`

Minds

Minds puts more emphasis on icons for sidebar navigation, yet it is still extremely effective in providing information to the user; it's website link is https://www.minds.com/

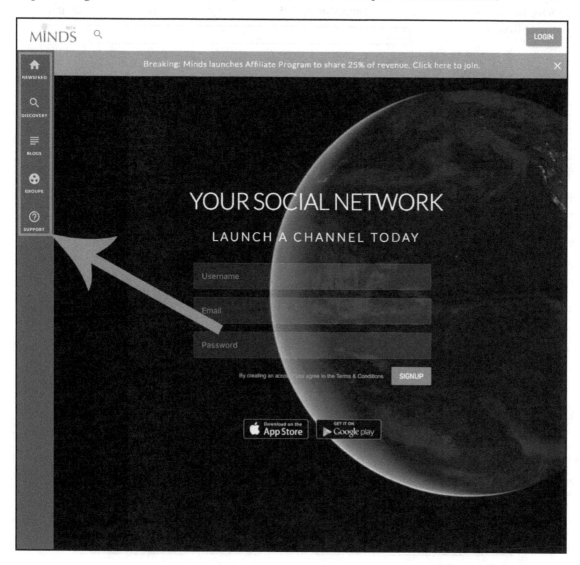

Myspace

Tom Anderson may be traveling the world taking amazing photos (check them out, they are truly amazing), but his social network lives on. Yes, it's not the top social network in the world, not by any means, but it constantly updates its design with a modern theme; it's website link is `https://myspace.com`

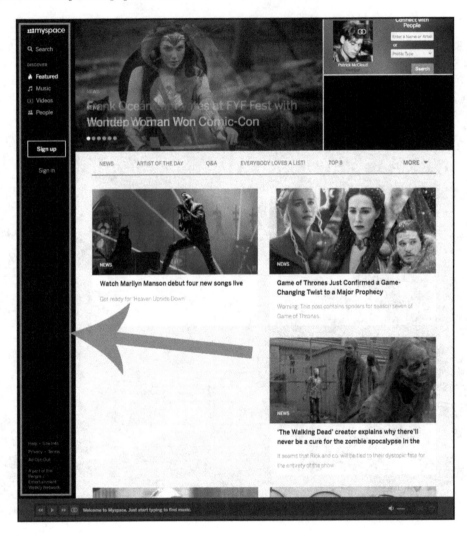

What will our social network sidebar consist of?

You're probably wondering what our social media sidebar will look like; it will contain the following:

- Links in the form of text
- Images for icons
- Responsive collapsible design

Although we implemented a sidebar in the preceding chapter, it was very basic and wasn't truly a sidebar in the conventional sense. Our sidebar will always be at the side; when the screen/browser is small, the sidebar will automatically hide and provide a burger button to show the sidebar. Yes, the button that shows and hides content like a sidebar with three horizontal lines is called a **burger button**.

Implementing the sidebar

Before we can start, we will need a base to work with. Luckily, in Chapter 7, *Creating the Blog Posts Homepage*, we did just this—we stripped away all code specific to the first project and used that as our base for the blog. Now, we can use that same base for the social network. If you do not have it, feel free to access it from the GitHub page.

 The sidebar that we will implement is based on the code from `https://www.codeply.com/go/8ES056VMns/bootstrap-4-sidebar-collapse/`

Implementing the burger button

Let's add it to our navigation bar. We won't link it with the sidebar yet because it does not exist, but it will be ready when the time for it comes later in this chapter.

First, we will include a style sheet called **Font Awesome**, which is great for really cool and useful icons using CSS. Add the following code to the HEADER.php file:

```
1  <!DOCTYPE html>
2  <html lang="en">
3    <head>
4      <!-- Required meta tags -->
5      <meta charset="utf-8">
6      <meta name="viewport" content="width=device-width,
         initial-scale=1, shrink-to-fit=no">
7
8      <!-- Bootstrap CSS -->
9      <link rel="stylesheet" href="https://
         maxcdn.bootstrapcdn.com/bootstrap/4.0.0-alpha.6/css/
         bootstrap.min.css" integrity="sha384rwResjU2yc3z8GV/
         NPeZWAv56rSmLldC3R/AZzGRnGxQQKnKkoFVMUwEyJ"
         crossorigin="anonymous">
10
11     <link rel="stylesheet" href="https://
         maxcdn.bootstrapcdn.com/font-awesome/4.7.0/css/
         font-awesome.min.css" />
12
13     <link rel="stylesheet" href="CSS/index.css" />
14   </head>
```

 A newer version of Font Awesome will work as well. For more information regarding Font Awesome, check out http://fontawesome.io/

Now that we can use cool icons, let's add a burger button. Consider the following navbar brand icon code:

```
15  <body>
16    <nav class="navbar navbar-toggleable-md navbar-inverse
      bg-inverse fixed-top">
17      <button class="navbar-toggler navbar-toggler-right"
        type="button" data-toggle="collapse" data-target="
        #navbarTogglerDemo02" aria-controls="
        navbarTogglerDemo02" aria-expanded="false" aria-label
        ="Toggle navigation">
18        <span class="navbar-toggler-icon"></span>
19      </button>
20
21      <a class="navbar-brand" href="index.php">
22        <img src="http://res.cloudinary.com/sonarsystems/
          image/upload/c_scale,w_150/v1442498022/
          Sonar-Systems-Circle-Logo_quet2k.png" width="30"
          height="30" alt="">
23      </a>
24
25      <div class="collapse navbar-collapse" id="
        navbarTogglerDemo02">
26        <ul class="navbar-nav mr-auto mt-2 mt-md-0">
27
28        </ul>
29
30        <form class="form-inline my-2 my-lg-0">
31          <input class="form-control mr-sm-2" type="text"
            placeholder="Search">
32
33          <button class="btn btn-outline-success my-2
            my-sm-0" type="submit">Search</button>
34        </form>
35      </div>
36    </nav>
```

Replace it with the following code:

```
<a href="#" id="SidebarToggle" data-target="#sidebar"
  data-toggle="collapse"><i class="fa fa-navicon
fa-2x py-2 p-1"></i></a>
```

The navigation bar will look like the following:

In the preceding code, we replaced our logo by simply creating a button, which targets an element with an `id` of sidebar, which we will implement soon. We use functionality from Font Awesome to retrieve the icon; for more information visit the Font Awesome website as mentioned earlier in this chapter.

Implementing the sidebar HTML side

Now that we have a button to show and hide the sidebar, we actually need a sidebar, otherwise the button is useless. Add the following code at the bottom of the HEADER.php file:

```
36    <div class="container-fluid">
37      <div class="row d-flex d-md-block flex-nowrap wrapper
        ">
38        <div class="col-md-3 float-left col-1 pl-0 pr-0
          collapse width show" id="sidebar">
39          <div class="list-group border-0 card text-center
            text-md-left">
40            <a href="#menu1" class="list-group-item
              d-inline-block collapsed" data-toggle="collapse
              " data-parent="#sidebar" aria-expanded="false">
              <i class="fa fa-dashboard"></i> <span class="
              hidden-sm-down">Account</span> </a>
41              <div class="collapse" id="menu1">
42                <a href="#" class="list-group-item"
                  data-parent="#menu1">Profile</a>
43                <a href="#" class="list-group-item"
                  data-parent="#menu1">Notifications</a>
44                <a href="#" class="list-group-item"
                  data-parent="#menu1">Messages</a>
45              </div>
46            <a href="#" class="list-group-item
              d-inline-block collapsed" data-parent="#sidebar
              "><i class="fa fa-film"></i> <span class="
              hidden-sm-down">Home</span></a>
47          </div>
48        </div>
49
50        <main class="col-md-9 float-left col px-5 pl-md-2
          pt-2 main">
```

Let's go over the code we just added:

- **Line 36** creates a container to store the sidebar and the page's main content.
- **Line 37** adds a row to store the content.
- **Line 38** creates a div to contain the sidebar, the classes applied should be all very straight forward.
- **Line 39** adds a div to store the list of items, which will be the buttons/items in the sidebar.
- **Line 40** adds a button, which is also a dropdown within the sidebar.
- **Line 41** adds the drop-down container.
- **Line 42** to **Line 44** adds the drop-down buttons/items.
- **Line 45** simply adds a button without any dropdown or other surprises.

- **Line 46** and **Line 47** close the sidebar and list group `div`.
- **Line 49** adds a container to store the main content of the page. When the screen size is medium or larger it is capped at a width of 9 columns, which allows the sidebar to be displayed next to it. On smaller screens, the sidebar is hidden by default.

You're probably thinking we haven't closed a few elements; that is correct. This is due to the fact that the main content is not in the header file but in another file, and the footer is also in another file. We will close off the elements after the footer in the `FOOTER.php` file, like so:

```
1   <footer class="footer">
2       <hr />
3
4       <div class="container">
5           <span>Awesome Footer 2017</span>
6       </div>
7   </footer>
8   </main>
9   </div>
10  </div>
11
12  <!-- jQuery first,      Tether, then Bootstrap JS. -->
13  <script src="https    /co   query.com/
        jquery-3.2.1.min.js  integri
        sha256-hwg4gsxgFZhOsEEamdOYGBf13           TwlAQgxVSNgt4="
        crossorigin="anonymous"></script>
14  <script src="https://cdnjs.cloudflare.com/ajax/libs/
        tether/1.4.0/js/tether.min.js" integrity="sha384-DztdAP
        BWPRXSA/3eYEEUWrWCy7G5KFbe8fFjk5JAIxUYHKkDx6Qin1DkWx51b
        Brb" crossorigin="anonymous"></script>
15  <script src="https://maxcdn.bootstrapcdn.com/
        bootstrap/4.0.0-alpha.6/js/bootstrap.min.js" integrity=
        "sha384-vBWWzlZJ8ea9aCX4pEW3rVHjgjt7zpkNpZk+02D9phzyeVk
        E+jo0ieGizqPLForn" crossorigin="anonymous"></script>
16
17  <script src="JS/index.js"></script>
18  </body>
19  </html>
```

This produces the following result:

The sidebar isn't much to look at, but it will be very soon. I urge you to resize your browser to see how the sidebar reacts to this change in size, a bit buggy but pretty cool even if I write so myself. Once the CSS is implemented, the sidebar will look and work a lot better.

 The icons next to the buttons are from the Font Awesome style sheet we included earlier in this chapter and were applied using classes.

Implementing the sidebar CSS side

We now have the HTML implemented, but it looks okay, sorry, it looks rubbish with no proper styling. Now, we will add the CSS to style the sidebar. Unlike the code we have added so far in this book where we would add a little bit and then run it, we will now add the entire code and then run it. The code will be added in chunks and explained because otherwise it wouldn't be legible to read if we put it all on one page, and it would be very overwhelming.

Start off by adding the following code to the bottom of the `index.css` file:

```css
#SidebarToggle
{
    color: white;
}

#sidebar
{
    overflow: hidden;
    z-index: 3;
    max-width: 250px;
}

#sidebar .list-group
{
    background-color: #333;
    min-height: 100vh;
}
```

The code we added does the following:

- The `#SidebarToggle` style: This makes the toggle sidebar button we added in the navigation menu white. Change this as you desire.
- The `#sidebar` style: This ensures that the sidebar is above the main content and restricts its width. The width is restricted as it would get larger and larger with the screen sizes width, which can begin to look ugly.

- The `#sidebar .list-group` style: This sets the background color and ensures that the sidebar is as tall as the web browser by using viewport units, which allow you to get a browser's current size—in this case, the height.

Let's add the next batch of code:

```
#sidebar i
{
  margin-right: 6px;
}

#sidebar .list-group-item
{
  border-radius: 0;
  background-color: #333;
  color: #ccc;
  border-left: 0;
  border-right: 0;
  border-color: #2c2c2c;
  white-space: nowrap;
}

#sidebar .list-group-item:not(.collapsed)
{
  background-color: #222;
}

#sidebar .list-group .list-group-item[aria-expanded="false"
    ]::after
{
  content: " \f0d7";
  font-family: FontAwesome;
  display: inline;
  text-align: right;
  padding-left: 5px;
}
```

The preceding code does the following:

- The `#sidebar i` style : This provides a small but effective gap between the icon and text in the sidebar.
- The `#sidebar .light-group-item` style: This provides a more fitting color scheme and style to the sidebar buttons/items. Feel free to change the colors to match your website's style.
- The `#sidebar .list-group-item:not(.collapsed)` style: This changes the background color of the sidebar item that is active (also known as opened). Feel free to change the color as usual.

- The `#sidebar .list-group .list-group-item[aria-expanded="false"]::after` style: This simply adds the arrow next to the drop-down item to indicate to the user that the item is a drop-down menu.

Lets add the next batch of code:

```
#sidebar .list-group .list-group-item[aria-expanded="true"]
{
    background-color: #222;
}

#sidebar .list-group .list-group-item[aria-expanded="true"]
    ::after
{
    content: " \f0da";
    font-family: FontAwesome;
    display: inline;
    text-align: right;
    padding-left: 5px;
}

#sidebar .list-group .collapse .list-group-item,
#sidebar .list-group .collapsing .list-group-item
{
    padding-left: 20px;
}

#sidebar .list-group .collapse > .collapse .list-group-item
    ,
#sidebar .list-group .collapse > .collapsing .
    list-group-item
{
    padding-left: 30px;
}
```

The preceding code does the following:

- The `#sidebar .list-group .list-group-item[aria-expanded="true"]` style: Changes the background color of the drop-down parent item.
- The `#sidebar .list-group .list-group-item[aria-expanded="true"]::after` style: Changes the drop-down arrow after it has been opened to show this change.
- The `#sidebar .list-group .collapse .list-group-item, #sidebar .list-group .collapsing .list-group-item` style: Sets how far drop-down menu items should be from the left.

- The `#sidebar .list-group .collapse > .collapse .list-group-item, #sidebar .list-group .collapse > .collapsing .list-group-item` style: Sets second-level drop-down menu items further to the right than first level. Although our menu does not have more than one level, it can easily be implemented, and this shows the styling behind it.

Let's add the next bit of code:

```css
@media (max-width:768px)
{
    #sidebar
    {
        min-width: 35px;
        max-width: 40px;
        overflow-y: auto;
        overflow-x: visible;
        transition: all 0.25s ease;
        transform: translateX(-45px);
        position: fixed;
    }

    #sidebar.show
    {
        transform: translateX(0);
    }

    #sidebar::-webkit-scrollbar
    {
        width: 0px;
    }

    #sidebar, #sidebar .list-group
    {
        min-width: 35px;
        overflow: visible;
    }
```

You may have noted that we started a media query but didn't close it off; this is due to there being more code that will be added in the next batch of code.

The styling is only applied to extra small and small screen sizes, as can be seen by the `max-width` condition. First, let's go over what the code we just added does:

- The `#sidebar` style: Sets the collapsed layout to show only icons
- The `#sidebar.show` style: Ensures that the collapsed menu is visible and on the left-hand side

- The `#sidebar::-webkit-scrollbar` style: Ensures that there is no scrollbar
- The `#sidebar, #sidebar .list-group` style: Sets a minimum width

Let's add the last batch of code to complete the media query:

```
#sidebar .list-group .collapse.show, #sidebar .
    list-group .collapsing
{
  position: relative;
  z-index: 1;
  width: 190px;
  top: 0;
}
#sidebar .list-group > .list-group-item
{
  text-align: center;
  padding: .75rem .5rem;
}

#sidebar .list-group > .list-group-item[aria-expanded=
    "true"]::after,
#sidebar .list-group > .list-group-item[aria-expanded=
    "false"]::after
{
  display:none;
}
}
```

The preceding code does the following:

- The `#sidebar .list-group .collapse.show, #sidebar .list-group .collapsing` style: Ensures that the drop-down menus are still positioned correctly
- The `#sidebar .list-group > .list-group-item` style: Ensures that the icons are positioned in the middle of the collapsed sidebar
- The `#sidebar .list-group > .list-group-item[aria-expanded="true"]::after, #sidebar .list-group > .list-group-item[aria-expanded="false"]::after` style: Ensures that the drop-down icons are hidden and not overlapping the main content

Now, let's add the final code:

```
.collapse.show
{
  visibility: visible;
}

.collapsing
{
  visibility: visible;
  height: 0;
  -webkit-transition-property: height, visibility;
  transition-property: height, visibility;
  -webkit-transition-timing-function: ease-out;
  transition-timing-function: ease-out;
}

.collapsing.width
{
  -webkit-transition-property: width, visibility;
  transition-property: width, visibility;
  width: 0;
  height: 100%;
  -webkit-transition-timing-function: ease-out;
  transition-timing-function: ease-out;
}
```

The last batch of code does the following:

- The `.collapse.show` style: Ensures that the menu is visible
- The `.collapsing` style: Ensures that the menu is visible and of the right size
- The `.collapsing.width` style: Ensures that the menu is visible and of the right size, similar to the style before it

We have now added all the code for the collapsible sidebar. There was a lot, so feel free to go over it again to ensure that you have everything and you completely understood it. Let's take a look at the fruits of our labor:

Looking good; let's take a look at what the sidebar looks like on smaller screen sizes:

The sidebar looks excellent; all the hard work has paid off.

 The best way—according to me—to see what a code does is to modify it and remove it temporarily and then see the result.

Summary

In this chapter, we covered adding a collapsible sidebar and started our social network project. The next chapter will cover implementing the home page in-line with the sidebar.

10
Creating the Home page in Our Social Network

In this chapter, we will continue with the social network project that we started in the preceding chapter. We will add the home page content to display a timeline of the user's social content. The timeline shows all the content the user has posted and also from other users they are following. This provides an excellent means for attracting the users when the website is first launched. This will be in conjunction with the previous chapters sidebar to provide a familiar layout.

In this chapter, the following topics will be covered:

- Bootstrap cards/tiles
- Bootstrap thumbnails
- Bootstrap sections
- Multiline text input
- Form input
- JavaScript AJAX form submission
- Debugging and testing responsive design

Social network timeline examples

Let's go through some examples of home pages/timelines in social networks. There are a plethora of social networks to get inspiration from. I'm sure that you have your own favorites, and I would always recommend that you check them out as well.

Facebook

Facebook is the most successful social network in human history, and most likely, every reader at some point has had a Facebook account; it is definitely one to take inspiration from. Facebook's main page isn't as responsive and modern as some of the other examples that we will look at, but it works. The website link for Facebook is `https://www.facebook.com/`

Google+

Google+ may not be the first social network you visit; however, with over 100 million active users and a consistently modern design, it deserves a place on our list. This timeline is responsive unlike Facebook's.

Let's take a look at its website link `https://plus.google.com/`:

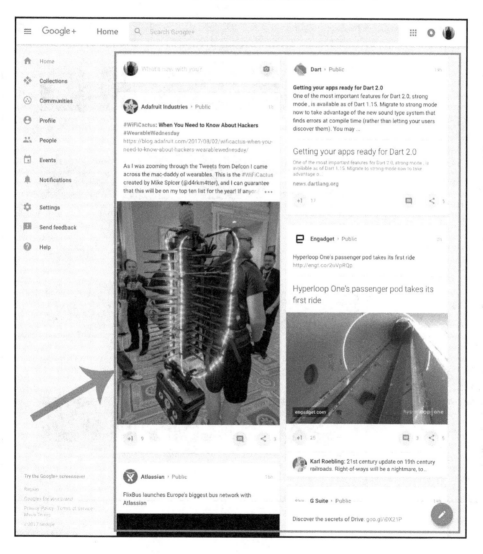

YouTube

YouTube's design has similarities to Google+ for obvious reasons, but it is used to display different information; it is responsive but not as responsive as Google+. This is due to it being more popular than Google+, and popular platforms have slower progression.

Let's take a look at its website link `https://www.youtube.com/`:

Twitter

Twitter uses a simple card system, similar to Google+, but the cards are placed one after another vertically.

Let's take a look at its website link `https://twitter.com/`:

Medium

Medium doesn't have a sidebar, so the entire page is the main content. It uses a mixture of jumbotron style banner and card system.

Let's take a look at its website link `https://medium.com/`:

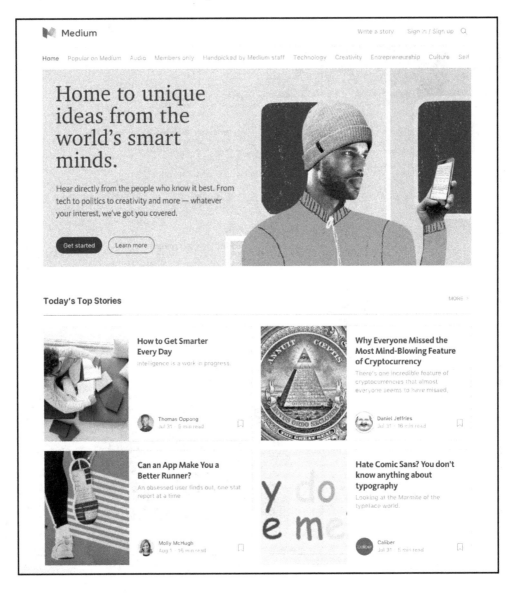

What will our social network timeline consist of?

You're probably wondering what our social media timeline will look like. We will use the Twitter-style layout, which was covered earlier; it will contain the following things:

- A multiline input field for posting content
- Bootstrap cards (similar to what we used in the blog homepage)
- Images
    - User thumbnail
    - Social post
- A singleline text to show username
- A singleline text to show the time content was posted
- A multiline text for post description
- Responsive design

We have already used cards in the blog, which worked amazingly by the way. We will implement them from the start again, as the layout will be slightly different. As usual, add your own twist to them using HTML elements and CSS to style them. Although Twitter's timeline isn't very responsive, ours will be; the content will simply shrink as the browser size changes.

Implementing the timeline

We will continue with the code from the preceding chapter, which implemented a fully working and collapsible sidebar.

The timeline consists of the following two main sections:

- The input section
- The timeline/feed section

Implementing the input section

The input field can vary from social media site to social media site, and how it appears can also vary. On Twitter, it is simple and always at the top of the page, but, on some websites, it can appear as a modal-style popup after some kind of add/post button is clicked on. We will keep things simple and use the Twitter style input field.

Add the following code to the index.php file:

```
1  <?php require_once( "SNIPPETS/HEADER.php" ); ?>
2
3  <div class="row">
4      <div class="col-12">
5          <form>
6              <div class="row">
7                  <div class="col-12">
8                      <label for="postDescription">Post
                        here...</label>
9                      <textarea class="form-control" id="
                        postDescription" rows="5"></textarea>
10                 </div>
11
12                 <div class="col-12" id="PostButtonContainer
                    ">
13                     <button type="submit" class="btn
                        btn-success col-12">Share To The World
                        </button>
14                 </div>
15             </div>
16         </form>
17     </div>
18 </div>
19
20 <?php require_once( "SNIPPETS/FOOTER.php" ); ?>
```

The code doesn't require too much description and is very similar to the contact form code from Chapter 6, *Creating a Contact Us Section*; the biggest difference being that there's only a single input field instead of multiple fields for name, email address, and so on. Let's take a look at the fruits of our clearly strenuous labor:

Looking good, but with just the same problem again: the button is directly below the input field. Adding a gap would help; it will look more visually appealing. Luckily, we have already added an `id` in the preceding code, called `PostButtonContainer`; simply add a margin at the top, like so:

```
#PostButtonContainer
{
    margin-top: 25px;
}
```

The preceding code produces the following result:

As you can see, this is significantly better than before. Feel free to modify the margin value as you see fit.

The input section is now complete, very simple. Next, we will move onto adding the main timeline feed using cards.

Implementing the timeline feed section

The timeline feed is pretty simple, but let's go over what it will consist of:

- The thumbnail image of the user who posted the social message
- The name of the user
- The main content, a mixture of text and images
- The time posted
- Social buttons using images/icons

Let's dive in and add the following code to your project:

```php
<?php require_once( "SNIPPETS/HEADER.php" ); ?>

<div class="row">
    <div class="col-12">
        <form>
            <div class="row">
                <div class="col-12">
                    <label for="postDescription">Post
                    here...</label>
                    <textarea class="form-control" id="
                    postDescription" rows="5"></textarea>
                </div>

                <div class="col-12" id="postButtonContainer
                ">
                    <button type="submit" class="btn
                    btn-success col-4">Share To The World
                    </button>
                </div>
            </div>
        </form>
    </div>
</div>

<div class="row">
    <div class="col-12">
        <div class="card">
            <div class="card-block">
                This text is awesome.
            </div>
        </div>
    </div>
</div>

<?php require_once( "SNIPPETS/FOOTER.php" ); ?>
```

Let's go through the preceding code:

- **Line 1** adds a row to store the timeline feed
- **Line 2** creates a timeline post container
- **Line 3** and **Line 4** create a card similar to the blog home page
- **Line 5** adds a simple text for the simple blog post

This produces the following result:

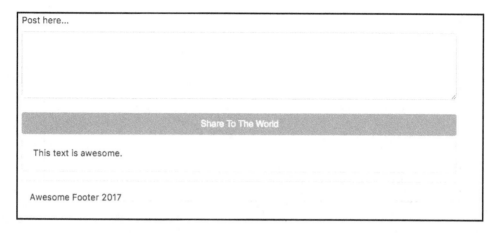

Again, the same issue persists as it has with every other project: there is no gap between the share button and the timeline post. We can remedy this using a margin. First, add a class of `postContainer` to the post container, like so:

```
<div class="row">
    <div class="col-12 postContainer">
        <div class="card">
            <div class="card-block">
                This text is awesome.
            </div>
        </div>
    </div>
</div>
```

Now, simply add margin to the class in the `index.css` file:

```
.postContainer
{
    margin-top: 10px;
}
```

This now produces the following result, which adds a gap above each timeline post:

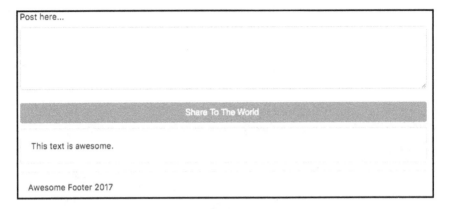

Adding the user's thumbnail image

Now that the container is created, let's add a thumbnail image for the user who has posted the content. Add the following code to the post:

```
<div class="row">
    <div class="col-12 postContainer">
        <div class="card">
            <div class="card-block">
                <div class="media">
                    <img class="d-flex mr-3" src="https://
                    t5.rbxcdn.com/
                    e96e5ea34a7af7ac1083f9c0d81de638">
                </div>
            </div>
        </div>
    </div>
</div>
```

Let's go over the new code line by line:

- **Line 1** adds a media object, which allows complex and repetitive components to be created especially when the media is positioned inline with content
- **Line 2** adds an image to act as the post user's thumbnail

The new code produces the following result:

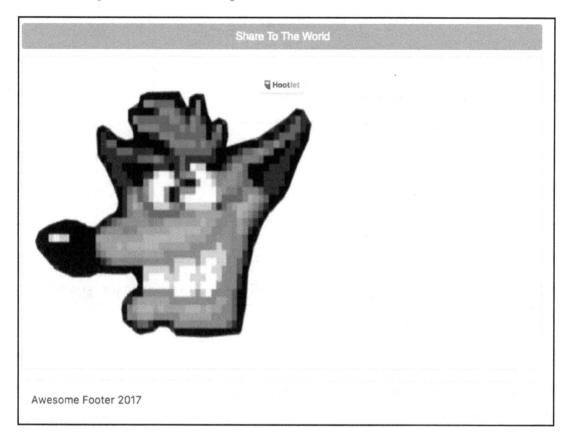

As you can see in the preceding screenshot, the thumbnail is too big, we can rectify this by manually setting the size of the image in CSS. First, we will need to add a class of postThumbnail, like so:

```
<div class="row">
    <div class="col-12 postContainer">
        <div class="card">
            <div class="card-block">
                <div class="media">
                    <img class="d-flex mr-3 postThumbnail"
                         src="https://t5.rb        com/
                         e96e5ea34a7af7ac1       c0d81de638">
                </div>
            </div>
        </div>
    </div>
</div>
```

Next, add the following style to the `index.css` file to restrict the size of the thumbnail:

```
.postThumbnail
{
    width: 100px;
}
```

As can be seen here, the thumbnail looks a lot better:

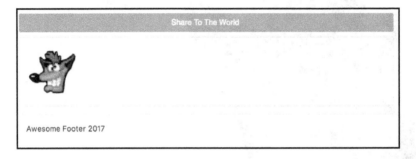

The thumbnail's height is automatically resized to maintain the ratio. Using a square for thumbnails is recommended to help keep consistency. Also, feel free to make the thumbnail smaller or larger.

Adding the user's name/username

We have a thumbnail of the user who posted the content; it would be awesome if we also showed the user's name. This can be simply done with some basic text, as follows:

```
<div class="row">
    <div class="col-12 postContainer">
        <div class="card">
            <div class="card-block">
                <div class="media">
                    <img class="d-flex mr-3 postThumbnail" src
                    ="https://t5.rbxcdn.com/
                    e96e5ea34a7af7ac1083f9c0d81de638">
                    <div class="media-body">
                        <h5 class="mt-0">Frahaan Hussain</h5>
                    </div>
                </div>
            </div>
        </div>
    </div>
</div>
```

Media body is a Bootstrap construct that extends the base media object, which allows a body to be added to our card. We now have the user's name displayed to the right of the thumbnail, as can be witnessed here:

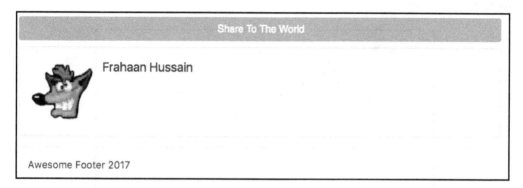

Adding the post's timestamp

It is very common for social posts in a timeline to have a timestamp that indicates when it was posted. This is very useful, as social networks are increasingly becoming sources of news for many people, hence a timestamp would allow the user to note how old the content/news they are consuming is.

Regarding where the timestamp should be situated, there are a few different common positions used:

- Next to the user's name, as in Twitter
- Below the user's name, as in Facebook
- At the bottom of the post, as in YouTube

Although we are using Twitter's overall layout, we will use Facebook's design for positioning the timestamp. It is good to study many different layouts and take different aspects to form the best layout possible. Add the following code below the user's name to display the timestamp:

```
<div class="row">
    <div class="col-12 postContainer">
        <div class="card">
            <div class="card-block">
                <div class="media">
                    <img class="d-flex mr-3 postThumbnail" src
                    ="https://t5.rbxcdn.com/
                    e96e5ea34a7af7ac1083f9c0d81de638">
                    <div class="media-body">
                        <h5 class="mt-0">Frahaan Hussain</h5>
                        <i>1st January 2000</i>
                    </div>
                </div>
            </div>
        </div>
    </div>
</div>
```

We use the italics tag to help distinguish the timestamp from the user's name. This produces the following result:

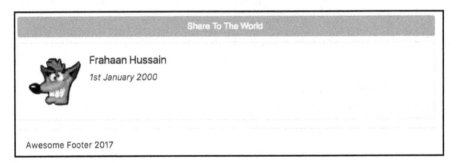

Adding the post's main body

We have almost finished the social post in the timeline; we just need to add the main body. We will use text, as follows:

```
<div class="media-body">
    <h5 class="mt-0">Frahaan Hussain</h5>
    <i>1st January 2000</i>

    <div>
        Lorem ipsum dolor sit amet,
        consectetur adipiscing elit, sed
        do eiusmod tempor incididunt ut
        labore et dolore magna aliqua. Ut
        enim ad minim veniam, quis
        nostrud exercitation ullamco
        laboris nisi ut aliquip ex ea
        commodo consequat. Duis aute
        irure dolor in reprehenderit in
        voluptate velit esse cillum
        dolore eu fugiat nulla pariatur.
        Excepteur sint occaecat cupidatat
        non proident, sunt in culpa qui
        officia deserunt mollit anim id
        est laborum.
    </div>
</div>
```

 I have used the Lorem Ipsum passage, but you may use anything you want.

This produces the following result:

Share To The World

Frahaan Hussain

1st January 2000

Lorem ipsum dolor sit amet, consectetur adipiscing elit, sed do eiusmod tempor incididunt ut labore et dolore magna aliqua. Ut enim ad minim veniam, quis nostrud exercitation ullamco laboris nisi ut aliquip ex ea commodo consequat. Duis aute irure dolor in reprehenderit in voluptate velit esse cillum dolore eu fugiat nulla pariatur. Excepteur sint occaecat cupidatat non proident, sunt in culpa qui officia deserunt mollit anim id est laborum.

Awesome Footer 2017

It looks good, but that wretched gap, or lack of one, is visually displeasing. As usual, we can easily rectify this; first, add a `postMainBody` class to the `div` we just added:

```
<div class="media-body">
    <h5 class="mt-0">Frahaan Hussain</h5>
    <i>1st January 2000</i>

    <div class="postMainBody">
        Lorem ipsum dolor sit amet,
        consectetur adipiscing elit, sed
        do eiusmod tempor incididunt ut
        labore et dolore magna aliqua. Ut
        enim ad minim veniam, quis
        nostrud exercitation ullamco
        laboris nisi ut aliquip ex ea
        commodo consequat. Duis aute
        irure dolor in reprehenderit in
        voluptate velit esse cillum
        dolore eu fugiat nulla pariatur.
        Excepteur sint occaecat cupidatat
        non proident, sunt in culpa qui
        officia deserunt mollit anim id
        est laborum.
    </div>
</div>
```

Now, add a margin to the top in the `index.css` file, like so:

```
.postMainBody
{
    margin-top: 15px;
}
```

As you can see in the following screenshot, the post looks a lot better:

Frahaan Hussain
1st January 2000

Lorem ipsum dolor sit amet, consectetur adipiscing elit, sed do eiusmod tempor incididunt ut labore et dolore magna aliqua. Ut enim ad minim veniam, quis nostrud exercitation ullamco laboris nisi ut aliquip ex ea commodo consequat. Duis aute irure dolor in reprehenderit in voluptate velit esse cillum dolore eu fugiat nulla pariatur. Excepteur sint occaecat cupidatat non proident, sunt in culpa qui officia deserunt mollit anim id est laborum.

Frahaan Hussain
1st January 2000

Lorem ipsum dolor sit amet, consectetur adipiscing elit, sed do eiusmod tempor incididunt ut labore et dolore magna aliqua. Ut enim ad minim veniam, quis nostrud exercitation ullamco laboris nisi ut aliquip ex ea commodo consequat. Duis aute irure dolor in reprehenderit in voluptate velit esse cillum dolore eu fugiat nulla pariatur. Excepteur sint occaecat cupidatat non proident, sunt in culpa qui officia deserunt mollit anim id est laborum.

Frahaan Hussain
1st January 2000

Lorem ipsum dolor sit amet, consectetur adipiscing elit, sed do eiusmod tempor incididunt ut labore et dolore magna aliqua. Ut enim ad minim veniam, quis nostrud exercitation ullamco laboris nisi ut aliquip ex ea commodo consequat. Duis aute irure dolor in reprehenderit in voluptate velit esse cillum dolore eu fugiat nulla pariatur. Excepteur sint occaecat cupidatat non proident, sunt in culpa qui officia deserunt mollit anim id est laborum.

I have added more social posts; this can easily be done by duplicating the `postContainer` class.

Going forward and extending the timeline

We are now done with the timeline. Although we didn't implement all of the features, we covered everything that will allow you to add extra features.

Take a look at the following extras and have a go yourself:

- Add responsive images/GIF to the main body
- Add responsive videos
- Add social icons for sharing
- Vary the content in each post

Summary

In this chapter, we added an awesome timeline to store all your social posts. We leveraged a variety of basic HTML features and Bootstrap features to implement this. In the next chapter, we will cover how to create a new page to display a user's profile page.

11

Creating the User's Profile Page

In this chapter, we will finish off our social network project. We will add a page to show a user's profile; this is essentially the page that would be available to other members. This will be used to display unique content for a particular user, such as information about them and content they have posted and/or interacted with.

In this chapter, the following topics will be covered:

- Bootstrap jumbotron
- Bootstrap cards
- A multiline text input
- Form input
- JavaScript AJAX form submission
- Debugging and testing responsive design

Social network profile examples

There are several social platforms to take inspiration from. Feel free to take a look at any favorites to discover ideas for a user profile page; alternatively, check out the examples from the previous chapter.

What will our social network user page consist of?

You're probably wondering what our social media user page will look like. We will use the Google+ style layout, which was covered earlier. Let's take a look at what the user page consists of:

- Jumbotron:
    - A user banner
    - The user's name
    - Extra information on the user, for example, their follower count
- Small cards to show what groups the user is following:
    - A banner image
    - A group name
    - The group member count
- Regular-sized cards to show the user's posts; these will be very similar to the timeline post cards

We used cards in the timeline as well. Cards are one of the many features of Bootstrap that you will constantly use, as they provide a very cool method for laying out content. As usual, add your own twist to them using HTML elements and CSS to style them. Google+'s user page is responsive, like the rest of the website; we too will follow suit.

Implementing the jumbotron

We will continue with the code from the preceding chapter, which extended the base with a timeline on the home page. We will first need to create a new page to store the user's profile page.

Create a new file in your root directory called `profile.php`. The project structure will now be as follows:

- CSS
- Images
- index.php

- JS
- `profile.php`
- SNIPPETS

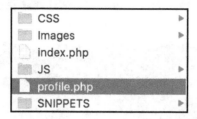

Now, we have our new file that will contain all of the user profile code. As usual, ensure that the PHP require code lines are placed inside the `profile.php` file.

Creating a basic jumbotron with a banner image

Let's create a basic jumbotron as we did in Chapter 4, *Creating the Introduction Section*, along with a banner image. Add the following code to the `profile.php` file:

```html
<div class="jumbotron jumbotron-fluid">
    <div class="row">
        <div class="col-12">
            <img src="https://
            lh3.googleusercontent.com/-ShX0GMbqg00/
            VH8qDnLhurI/AAAAAAAAAas/
            sJvfY7eWOp0ZI9YFffcOhwRtPgDGc_JhgCL0BGAYYCw/
            s1000-fcrop64=1,01ab0000ffa9ffff/
            Youtube%2Bnew%2Bheader.png" />
        </div>
    </div>
</div>
```

The code we added is nothing new; we have used this before. Let's take a look at jumbotron's result:

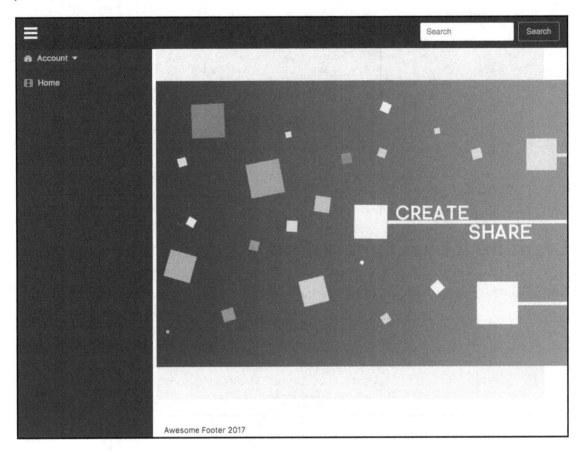

As usual, the code never works the first time. As can be seen from the preceding screenshot, there are two problems, as follows:

- The image overflows and needs to be restricted to the jumbotron's width
- There is padding at the top and bottom, which is very unappealing

Luckily, these are simple fixes, and we have actually done these several times over. I would recommend that you tackle them yourself before looking at the steps that follow. First, we will need to add an `id` of `ProfileJumbotron` to the `jumbotron div`:

```
<div id="ProfileJumbotron" class="jumbotron jumbotron-fluid
">
    <div class="row">
        <div class="col-12">
            <img src="https://
            lh3.googleusercontent.com/-ShX0GMbqg00/
            VH8qDnLhurI/AAAAAAAAAas/
            sJvfY7eWOp0ZI9YFffcOhwRtPg_c_JhgCL0BGAYYCw/
            s1000-fcrop64=1,01ab0000ffa9ffff/
            Youtube%2Bnew%2Bheader.png" />
        </div>
    </div>
</div>
```

Now, add the following code to the `index.css` file to remove padding, which will remove the gray parts and add a small margin, which is optional (I like it):

```
#ProfileJumbotron
{
    padding-bottom: 0;
    padding-top: 0;
    margin-top: 5px;
}
```

This removes the gray parts, as can be seen here:

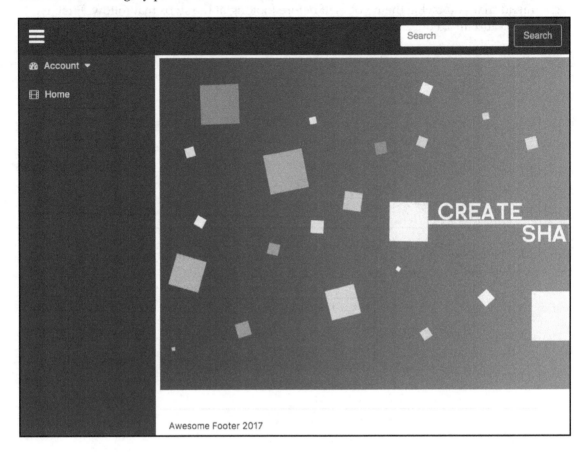

However, the image overflows, as it isn't responsive; let's solve this. First, add an `id` of `ProfileBannerImage` to the image:

```
<div id="ProfileJumbotron" class="jumbotron jumbotron-fluid
">
    <div class="row">
        <div class="col-12">
            <img id="ProfileBannerImage" src="https://
            lh3.googleusercontent.com/-ShX0GMbqg00/
            VH8qDnLhurI/AAAAAAAAAas/
            sJvfY7eWOp0ZI9YFffcOhwRtPgDGc_JhgCL0BGAYYCw/
            s1000-fcrop64=1,01ab0000ffa9ffff/
            Youtube%2Bnew%2Bheader.png" />
        </div>
    </div>
</div>
```

Now, add the following styling code to the `index.css` file to restrict the width of the image to the jumbotron's width:

```
#ProfileBannerImage
{
    width: 100%;
}
```

Now, the image is nice and responsive and is restricted to the size of the jumbotron:

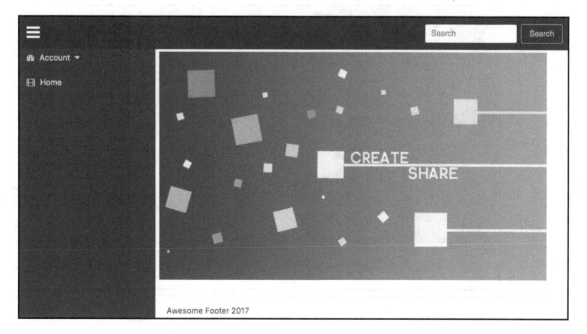

Adding the overlay text

We have a basic jumbotron setup; let's add a text overlay to display the user's name and their follower count. Add the following code below the image:

```
<div id="ProfileJumbotron" class="jumbotron jumbotron-fluid">
    <div class="row">
        <div class="col-12">
            <img id="ProfileBannerImage" src="http://
            lh3.googleusercontent.com/-ShX0GMbqg/
            VH8qDnLhurI/AAAAAAAAAas/
            sJvfY7eWOp0ZI9YFffcOhwRtPgDGo_Jhg0BGAYYCw/
            s1000-fcrop64=1,01ab0000ffa9f
            Youtube%2Bnew%2Bheader.png" /
            <h3>
                Sonar Systems
            </h3>

            <p>
                1,000,000,000 Follows :D
            </p>
        </div>
    </div>
</div>
```

Let's take a look at our amazing jumbotron; do you want to put a bet on whether or not it will work the first time?

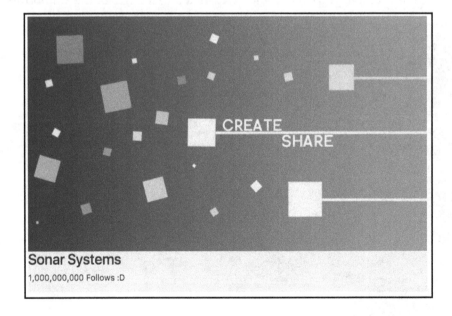

The text is not overlaid. Don't worry, no need to pull your hair out. This is easily rectified, we won't even have to add any extra CSS code. We can borrow a class from the carousel functionality within Bootstrap, and simply enclose the text we just added within a `div` with a class of `carousel-caption`:

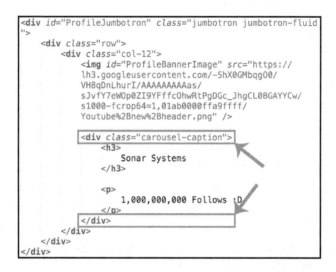

This produces the following result:

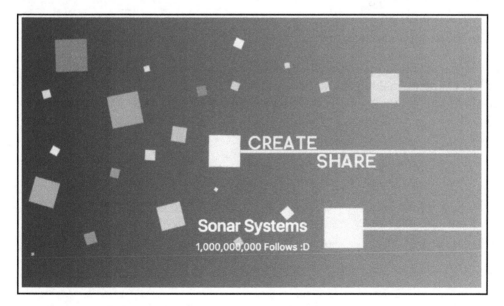

We are now done with the jumbotron but there are plenty of extras we can add to the jumbotron. The following are some examples; add these extras, which you can implement as an extra task:

- The user's thumbnail image
- Buttons:
  - Edit
  - About
- Extras text
- Positioning the overlaid content

Implementing the small cards

We will now implement cards to showcase the user's interests and groups they are following. This is extremely useful as a snapshot for other users to see what a particular user is into without having to converse with them.

We will use cards again; this time they will be a lot smaller, as they don't need to display as much information. They simply need to display the following content:

- The banner image
- The group name
- The group member count

This will be extremely simple and will reuse techniques we have already implemented over the last few chapters, making this an ideal feature for you to tackle yourself. If you want a hint, check out the following code, which goes after the `jumbotron div` container:

```
21  <div class="row">
22      <div class="col-lg-3 col-6 cardContainer">
23        <div class="card">
24          <a href="post.php"><img class="card-img-top
            cardImage" src="https://
            lh3.googleusercontent.com/-t7s6QT-8e30/AAAAAAAAAAI/
            AAAAAAAAAAA/sX5duDFyQ5s/w320-h180-p-rw/photo.jpg"
            alt="Card image cap"></a>
25
26          <div class="card-block">
27            <a href="post.php"><h4 class="card-title">
              Interest 1</h4></a>
28
29            <p class="card-text">1000 Members</p>
30          </div>
31        </div>
32      </div>
33  </div>
```

There is no need to explain this code again, as we have used cards multiple times. Also, this is almost identical to the card system used in Chapter 7, *Creating the Blog Posts Homepage*, for the blog home page, so feel free to go back if you are unsure about anything.

 cardContainer and cardImage are custom classes, which were implemented in Chapter 7, *Creating the Blog Posts Homepage*.

The only difference in terms of HTML structure is the column sizes used. This card system will display four on a single row if the screen is big enough instead of three, as these cards aren't the main staple point of the page. Also, the minimum number of cards on a single row will be two on smaller screen sizes. If you need a refresher on Bootstrap's grid system, then feel free to return to Chapter 2, *What is Bootstrap, Why Do We Use It?*.

Let's take a look at the fruits of our labor:

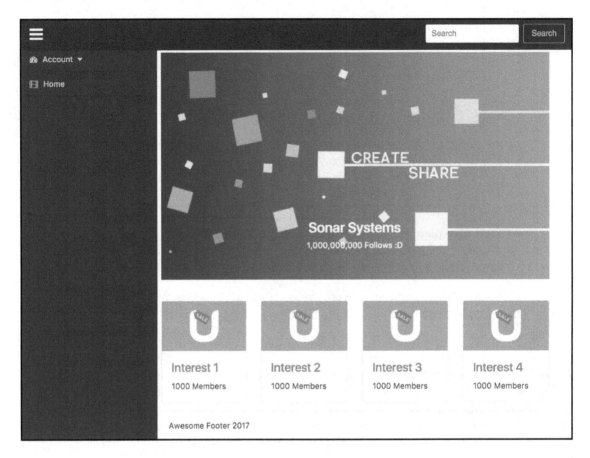

I have added extra cards, which can simply be achieved by duplicating the code within the `row div` and changing any information that is needed for each of the user's interests.

Here are some extra tasks to extend the interest cards:

- Title
- Vary the images and information for each interest tile

Implementing the large cards

We have almost completed the profile page; the only thing left is to add the user's posts. We will actually reuse the code from the home page, as the posts will look the same, the only difference being the cards will not be stored solely on a single row but two will be stored on the same row on larger screens.

Before taking a look at the following code for adding the postcards, try making the change yourself:

```
<div class="row">
    <div class="col-lg-6 col-12 postContainer">
        <div class="card">
            <div class="card-block">
                <div class="media">
                    <img class="d-flex mr-3 postThumbnail"
                    src="https://t5.rbxcdn.com/
                    e96e5ea34a7af7ac1083f9c0d81de638">

                    <div class="media-body">
                        <h5 class="mt-0">Frahaan Hussain</
                        h5>
                        <i>1st January 2000</i>

                        <div class="postMainBody">
                            Lorem ipsum dolor sit amet,
                            consectetur adipiscing elit,
                            sed do eiusmod tempor
                            incididunt ut labore et
                            dolore magna aliqua.
                        </div>
                    </div>
                </div>
            </div>
        </div>
    </div>
</div>
```

The following changes were made to the post cards from the preceding page:

- Added a col-lg-6 class to the post container to ensure that there are two posts on a single row on larger screens
- Reduced the amount of text in the post main body; this was just to ensure that the preceding code snapshot doesn't occupy too much space

This all leads to the following end result:

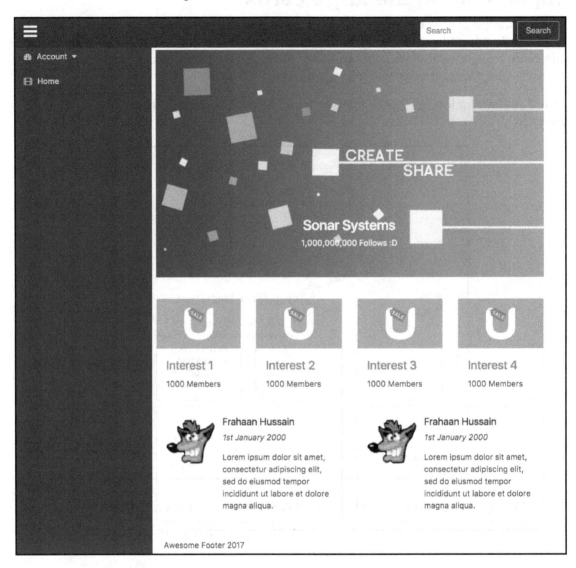

Now, we are done not just with this page but this project, woohoo! What we haven't done is link this page to the site's navigation and/or other page(s); I will leave that as an extra task for you.

 The preceding code only showed a single card being added; I duplicated it as we did in the preceding chapter to demonstrate what it would look like with more than one.

Summary

In this chapter, we created the user's profile page; which incorporated a wide variety of features that we learned throughout this book thus far. In the next chapter, we will kick-start our fourth and final project. I'll see you there.

12
Displaying Thumbnails of Our Photos

In this chapter, we will start our fourth and final project: a photo gallery. This chapter will cover creating the home page as usual, only this time the home page will be used to display small previews of photos. We will incorporate many of the skills that we learned over the previous chapters and some cool new ones.

The topics to be covered in this chapter are as follows:

- Bootstrap image showcase
- CSS styling
- Bootstrap buttons
- Bootstrap pagination
- Debugging and testing responsive design

Photo gallery home page examples

Let's go through some examples of photo gallery home pages. There are a plethora of photo galleries to choose to get inspiration from. I'm sure that you have your own favorites, and I would always recommend that you check them out as well if they are not covered over the next few pages.

Pinterest

Pinterest is the one of the most successful photo galleries in the world, and most likely you have already visited it. It is definitely one to take inspiration from. Pinterest uses a masonry –style effect to lay out the images using cards. The website is responsive on medium to extra large screen sizes. It makes full use of the browser's width using a fluid-like design.

Let's take a look at its website (`https://www.pinterest.co.uk/`):

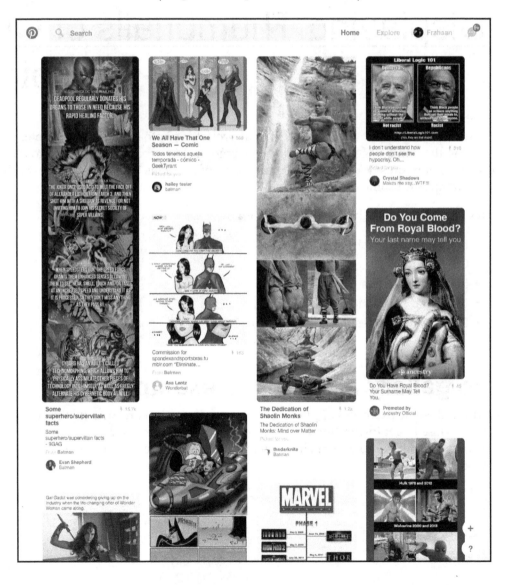

9GAG

9GAG is a very popular website for funny images. It's not the conventional photo gallery, but a blend of Facebook and a normal photo gallery. 9GAG is not responsive, one of the reasons being that they have an app that they would like users to download. Never make this mistake; always ensure that your website is fully responsive as well, because some users won't want to download an extra app.

Let's take a look at its website (`https://9gag.com/`):

Google Photos

Google keeps on giving. It pretty much has a platform for every idea. However, Google Photos isn't like a conventional photo gallery in that it is private and primarily designed to store and showcase your own photos. It has an excellent and responsive layout that borrows from the greatest Google websites and provides simplicity.

Let's take a look at its website link (`https://photos.google.com/`):

GIPHY

GIPHY is very much like 9GAG. It provides images, or more specifically GIFs, for community amusement. However, it doesn't provide a responsive layout, which is a shame. The interface is minimal with no sidebar, captions, or cards like Pinterest's design.

Let's take a look at its website (`https://giphy.com/`):

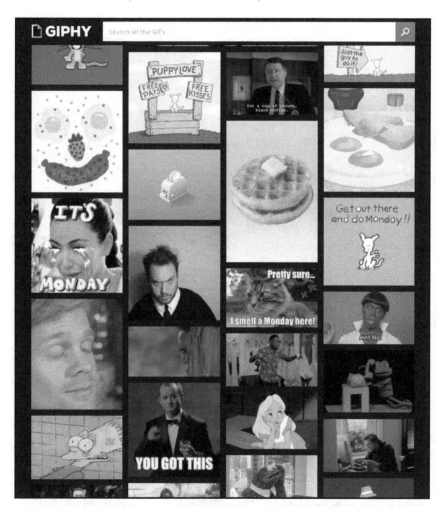

Vent

Vent is a fairly new and relatively unheard of photo gallery. It also provides the feature of allowing text-based posts, so it is unique in that fashion. It uses a fully responsive website along with cards to display content tagged with an emotion.

Let's take a look at its website (`http://www.ventit.co/`):

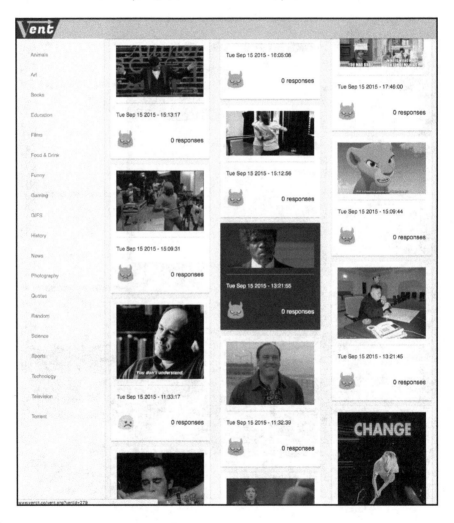

What will our photo gallery home page consist of?

You're probably wondering what our photo gallery sidebar will look like. It will contain the following:

- Title for the page
- Thumbnails/images in the form of files
- Pagination (navigation for multipage thumbnails)

Photo galleries are usually very simple, and ours will be no different. We will omit a sidebar, but you can easily use the code from the previous project to incorporate a sidebar into our photo gallery and make it look more like Google Photos.

Implementing the thumbnails

Before we can start, we will need a base to work with. Luckily, in `Chapter 7`, *Creating the Blog Posts Home Page*, we did just this; we stripped away all code specific to the first project and used that as our base for the blog. Now, we can use that same base for the photo gallery. The code files can be accessed easily via the GitHub repository.

Adding the home page title

There is nothing special about the title we are going to add and it is extremely simple to implement, as demonstrated here:

```php
1  <?php require_once( "SNIPPETS/HEADER.php" ); ?>
2
3  <div class="container">
4      <div class="row">
5          <div class="col-12 text-center">
6              <h1>The Best Photo Gallery In The World</h1>
7          </div>
8      </div>
9  </div>
10
11 <?php require_once( "SNIPPETS/FOOTER.php" ); ?>
```

We aren't doing anything new in the preceding code; we are just creating a simple container with a row. Inside, we have a container for the title that spans all 12 columns and centers the content with it, ensuring that our title will always be in the center.

This code produces the following result:

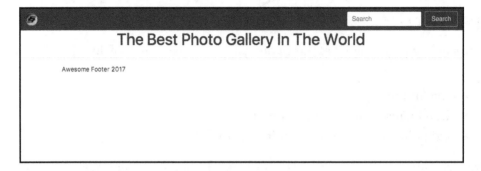

Adding the picture thumbnails

Now, we will add the main part of our website, the array of thumbnails, which when clicked enlarge to show the image in all its glory. Add the following code below the previously added code snippet:

```php
1  <?php require_once( "SNIPPETS/HEADER.php" ); ?>
2
3  <div class="container">
4      <div class="row">
5          <div class="col-12 text-center">
6              <h1>The Best Photo Gallery In The World</h1>
7          </div>
8      </div>
9
10     <div class="row">
11         <div class="col-lg-2 col-md-3 col-sm-6 col-12">
12             <img src="http://res.cloudinary.com/dmliyxggm
                   /image/upload/v1511804166/photo1_bcjm1j.jpg"
                   class="img-thumbnail">
13         </div>
14     </div>
15 </div>
16
17 <?php require_once( "SNIPPETS/FOOTER.php" ); ?>
```

In the preceding code snippet, first we added a row, nothing special there. Next, we added a `div` to contain the thumbnail image. It has a variety of breakpoints to aid the layout; this ensures that items are always legible on all screen sizes. Finally, we added an image with a Bootstrap thumbnail image class, which is designed to be responsive, and put a border around it. Let's take a look at our result:

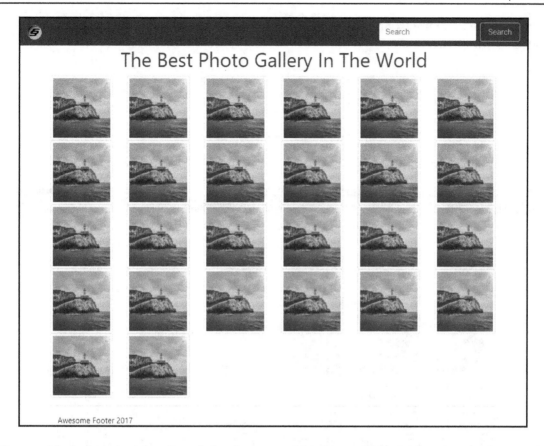

I have added extra thumbnails to help showcase what it would look like. This can be simply achieved by duplicating the div that contains the image, *not the row* div. You would obviously want to change the images for more variety and more importantly authenticity; do this as an extra task to see what it looks like. I can assure you that it will look epic.

There is one little problem, which you guessed correctly. There is no gap between the tiles on the top and bottom; we can easily overcome this by adding a margin to the top and bottom of each image. First, add a class of thumbnailContainer, as follows:

```
10    <div class="row">
11        <div class="col-lg-2 col-md-3 col-sm-6 col-12
          thumbnailContainer">
12            <img src="http://res.cloudinary.com/dmliyxggm
              /image/upload/v1511804166/photo1_bcjm1j.jpg"
              class="img-thumbnail">
13        </div>
```

Now, add the following style code to `index.css`, which applies a margin to the top and bottom of the container:

```
.thumbnailContainer
{
    margin-top: 5px;
    margin-bottom: 5px;
}
```

Let's take a look at our page now:

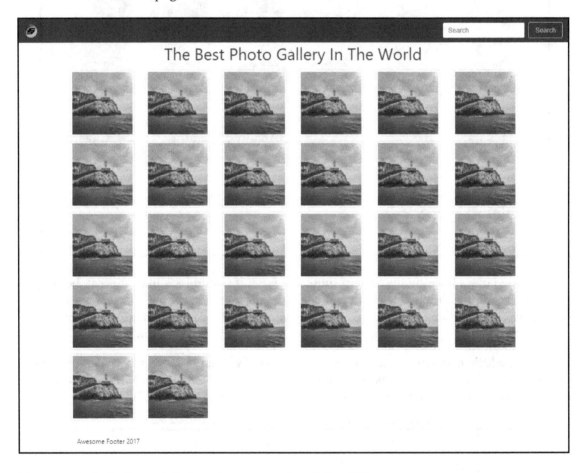

Now our website is much better; the gaps make all the difference.

Adding pagination

Pagination is completely new to us, so what is it? **Pagination** simply provides links that indicate a series of related content that exists across multiple pages. This is typically used as means to improve performance instead of potentially showing millions of posts on a single page.

Take a look at the screenshot of pagination at work:

 The number of pages cannot be determined in advance. They would be dynamically calculated, depending on the amount of content stored in a database.

The preceding screenshot is from ventit.co, which was provided as an example earlier on. Implementing pagination couldn't be simpler; add the following code after the thumbnail grid row:

```
<div class="row">
    <div class="col-12 text-center">
        <nav>
            <ul class="pagination">
                <li class="page-item"><a class="page-link" href="#">Previous</a></li>
                <li class="page-item"><a class="page-link" href="#">1</a></li>
                <li class="page-item"><a class="page-link" href="#">2</a></li>
                <li class="page-item"><a class="page-link" href="#">3</a></li>
                <li class="page-item"><a class="page-link" href="#">Next</a></li>
            </ul>
        </nav>
    </div>
</div>
```

Let's go through the code line by line:

- **Line 1** adds a row like we have done many times before
- **Line 2** adds a div to contain the pagination, which will span all 12 columns on all screen sizes
- **Line 3** creates a navigation system for the pagination

- **Line 4** creates an unordered list with the pagination class, which will contain

each button for the pagination navigation
- **Line 5** to **Line 9** add the individual buttons

 You would want to link the buttons to the appropriate pages using the `href` in a working example, which has a backend as well.

Let's take a look at what it looks like:

We added the `text-center` class, so why is the pagination not centered? Well, it requires a different display style. To change the display style, first add an `id` of `PaginationList`, as follows:

```
<div class="row">
    <div class="col-12 text-center">
        <nav>
            <ul class="pagination" id="PaginationList">
                <li class="page-item"><a class="page-l      href="#">Previous</a></li>
                <li class="page-item"><a class="page-li      href="#">1</a></li>
                <li class="page-item"><a class="page-lik"   f="#">2</a></li>
                <li class="page-item"><a class="page-link" hre  #">3</a></li>
                <li class="page-item"><a class="page-link" href=" ">Next</a></li>
            </ul>
        </nav>
    </div>
</div>
```

Now, add the following CSS code to the index.css file:

```
#PaginationList
{
    display: inline-flex;
}
```

The new display layout produces this new result:

We are now done with the pagination system and can move on to the final chapter of this project and book.

 Pagination can be customized in a variety of ways using arrows, instead of the **Previous** and **Next** text buttons to highlight and disable buttons; more information can be found on the Bootstrap website at `https://v4-alpha.getbootstrap.com/components/pagination/`

Summary

In this chapter, we started our fourth and final project: the photo gallery. We implemented the home page, which displayed a grid of thumbnails.

The next chapter will cover opening the images up when they are clicked on.

13
Opening Images Using a Light Box

In this chapter, we will finish our final project, the photo gallery. This chapter will cover extending the gallery thumbnails on the home page. We won't create a new page, but instead show extra contextual information. We will use some cool features to bring our light box to life, allowing full viewing of the images that were previously only previewed to us via the grid.

The topics covered in this chapter are as follows:

- Bootstrap modals
- Form input
- Multiline text input
- CSS page darkening
- Debugging and testing responsive design

Light box examples

Let's go through some examples of excellent light boxes. There are a plethora of light boxes to choose to get inspiration from. I'm sure that you have your own favorites, and I would always recommend that you check them out as well if they are not covered over the next few pages.

Pinterest

Pinterest is one of the most successful photo galleries in the world, and most likely you have already visited it—it is definitely one to take inspiration from. Pinterest hides all the other content to showcase the image. The light box is fully responsive:

Its website is https://www.pinterest.co.uk/

Google Photos

Google Photos opens the image in full to maximize the visual effect. Google also offers some extra editing buttons, as it is a private gallery and not a public one, so certain aspects will vary from other photo galleries:

Its website is `https://photos.google.com/`

Dan Kennedy

Dan Kennedy is an amazing photographer, and his website is an example of minimalism done right. The visual esthetic is very pleasing and also very effective in conveying information to the user:

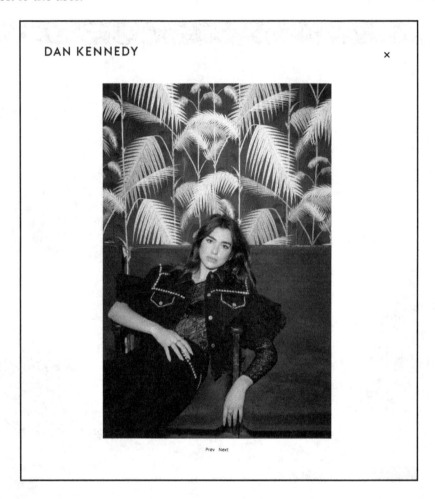

Its website is http://www.danielkennedy.com/

Salter

Salter is really cool in that it doesn't remove/hide all the website's content, but instead incorporates the sidebar and merely maximizes the image to cover the thumbnails and not the entire page:

Its website is https://www.jefferysalter.com/

Arild Danielsen Photographer

Arild Danielsen Photography is similar to the other examples we have covered, but with a twist. Open the page up hover over an open image, and see what happens. The image zooms in and allows you to pan using the mouse, which is really cool.

Take a look at its website at http://www.danielsenphoto.com/portfolio_editorial.html

What will our light box consist of?

First of all, what exactly is a light box outside of it's photography origins? It sounds extremely cool, almost as cool as a jumbotron. A light box is an extremely simple concept. When an object is clicked on, usually a smaller object in the midst of many like itself, displayed as a preview, the object opens up to showcase itself in all its glory. In the case of our photo gallery, when the thumbnail in the grid is clicked, the image will open up to fill most, if not all, of the browser.

You're probably wondering what our light box will look like; it will contain the following:

- A full–size image
- A close button
- Text to briefly describe the image and provide some contextual information to the user

Implementing the light box

We will continue with the code from the preceding chapter to finish our photo gallery with an awesome light box.

We will use a Bootstrap feature called **modals**, which is an awesome and simple way of opening a box within the website; this is what will display our image to the user.

Adding a simple modal

First, we will open an empty modal when the thumbnail is clicked from the gallery. Add the following code after all other HTML code, even outside of the container:

```
<div class="modal fade" role="dialog" id="LightBoxModal" aria-hidden="true">
    <div class="modal-dialog" role="document">
        <div class="modal-content">
            <div class="modal-header">
                <h5 class="modal-title">Modal title</h5>
                <button type="button" class="close" data-dismiss="modal"
                aria-label="Close">
                    <span aria-hidden="true">&times;</span>
                </button>
            </div>
        </div>
    </div>
</div>
```

Firstly, I'm sure you're wondering why we added it outside of the container and not within it, considering everything thus far in the book has been within. The main reason for this is due to the code not being part of the main visible content, so it doesn't need to be within the container. It can be placed within the container, but honestly there is no need. Before we go over what each line of code does, let's take a look at the end result:

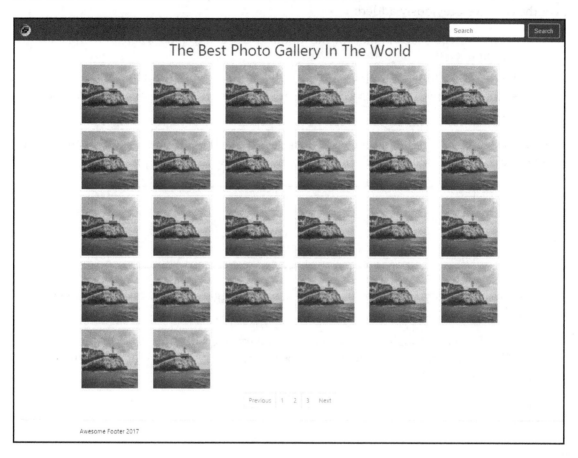

No, you're not mistaken; the website looks exactly the same. This is because the purpose of a modal is to remain hidden until triggered, at which point it will appear and take away focus from the rest of the website by making it slightly gray/dark. So, how do we trigger the modal? Well, it will be triggered by clicking on a thumbnail image from the grid; however, as of now this does not work, as we haven't implemented a trigger. Before we do so, let's go over the code we previously added:

- **Line 1** creates a container for the modal and sets it to fade when showing and hiding itself
- **Line 2** and **Line 3** set up the inner container to actually store the modal
- **Line 4** creates a header section to provide a title for the modal and a button to close it

Now that we have covered what the code does, let's make the thumbnails trigger the modal when clicked. Simply extend the thumbnail image with the following properties:

```
<div class="col-lg-2 col-md-3 col-sm-6 col-12
thumbnailContainer">
    <img src="http://res.cloudinary.com/dmliyxggm/image/upload
    /v1511804166/photo1_bcim1j.jpg" class="img-thumbnail"
    data-toggle="modal" data-target="#LightBoxModal">
</div>
```

These properties specify what type of content is being triggered based on an ID, which is our modal.

 Each thumbnail image will need to be updated like this. Luckily, the code is the same, and a new modal doesn't need to be created for each new thumbnail image.

When one of the thumbnail images from the grid is clicked, the following appears:

Adding an image to the modal

The main reason we are implementing a modal is to showcase the image the user has clicked. However, at the moment nothing but a title is displayed; we will keep that as it is also useful, but what we really need is an image. Luckily for us, it is extremely simple; add the following code to the modal:

```
<div class="modal fade" role="dialog" id="LightBoxModal" aria-hidden="true">
    <div class="modal-dialog modal-lg" role="document">
        <div class="modal-content">
            <div class="modal-header">
                <h5 class="modal-title" id="ImageTitle">Modal Title</h5>
                <button type="button" class="close" data-dismiss="modal"
                aria-label="Close">
                    <span aria-hidden="true">&times;</span>
                </button>
            </div>
            <div class="modal-body">
                <img class="img-thumbnail" src="http://res.cloudinary.com/
                dmliyxggm/image/upload/v1511804166/photo1_bcjm1j.jpg" />
            </div>
        </div>
    </div>
</div>
```

I think you can guess what the div we added does; it provides a section to put the main content for the modal in. For our purposes, it will just be an image, but I recommend as an extra task that you add some text to further describe the image; you could also implement a footer for extra content. You can check out all the features of Bootstrap modals at https://v4-alpha.getbootstrap.com/components/modal/

Inside of the body, we will simple add an image with the thumbnail class, which ensures that it is responsive and fills the width of its parent container while maintaining its native aspect ratio. Let's take a look at the end result:

It looks cool, but a light box should showcase the image in all its glory—I think the modal should be bigger and better. As per usual, Bootstrap keeps on giving; there is a class we can add to the modal dialog `div` to change its size. Add a class of `modal-lg`, as follows:

```
<div class="modal fade" role="dialog" id="LightBoxModal" aria-hidden="true">
    <div class="modal-dialog modal-lg" role="document">
        <div class="modal-content">
            <div class="modal-header">
                <h5 class="modal-title" id="ImageTitle">Modal title</h5>
                <button type="button" class="close" data-dismiss="modal"
                aria-label="Close">
                    <span aria-hidden="true">&times;</span>
                </button>
            </div>

            <div class="modal-body">
                <img class="img-thumbnail" src="http://res.cloudinary.com/
                dmliyxggm/image/upload/v1511804166/photo1_bcjm1j.jpg" />
            </div>
        </div>
    </div>
</div>
```

 If you want to make the modal smaller, you can add a class of `modal-sm`.

This is what the larger modal looks like:

As you can see in the preceding screenshot, the modal being bigger really makes our light box stand out to the user. It fully expresses the image in all its glory.

Making the modal content appear dynamically

Technically, we are done with the modal and the book. Like I said, technically we could leave it as it is, but let's make it more dynamic. At the moment, when we click on a thumbnail image, the same modal with the same image and information is displayed. We don't want multiple modals, as that leads to a lot of redundancy. This is something we have tried to avoid throughout this book; we cannot give up this ideology now that we stand near the finishing line.

That's where dynamic content comes into play. We will use JavaScript to perform the following tasks:

1. Check when a thumbnail image has been clicked (override the default functionality)
2. Retrieve the thumbnail's data:
   - Image
   - Title (to be added to the image)
   - Anything else you may want
3. Replace the content of the modal
4. Show the modal

Using these steps, we will be able to dynamically switch the modal's content nice and seamlessly. All of our thumbnails have the same image—that's fine, because in a production website, this would not be the case, and the code we will add will provide us with the means of handling the different images dynamically and accordingly.

First, we will remove all data–toggle and targets from every image. This might sound counter-intuitive, as it was the very code that opened the modal. This hardcoded method is great for modals that are static, but we want to dynamically change the content. So, we will override the functionality in JavaScript by detecting when an image has been clicked and opening the modal with its attributes.

Consider all images in the following code:

```
<div class="col-lg-2 col-md-3 col-sm-6 col-12 thumbnailContainer">
    <img src="http://res.cloudinary.com/dmliyxggm/image/upload/
    v1511804166/photo1_bcjm1j.jpg" class="img-thumbnail" data-toggle=
    "modal" data-target="#LightBoxModal">
</div>
```

Now, make the following changes:

```
<div class="col-lg-2 col-md-3 col-sm-6 col-12 thumbnailContainer">
    <img src="http://res.cloudinary.com/dmliyxggm/image/upload/
    v1511804166/photo1_bcjm1j.jpg" class="img-thumbnail">
</div>
```

The modal does not appear when you click on any of the thumbnails. Now, add a class of
`thumbnailImage` to each image, like so:

```
<div class="col-lg-2 col-md-3 col-sm-6 col-12
thumbnailContainer">
    <img src="http://res.cloudinary.com/dmliyxggm
    /image/upload/v1511804166/photo1_bcjm1j.jpg"
    class="img-thumbnail thumbnailImage">
</div>
```

This will act as the handle for detecting the click in JavaScript. Before we implement the
JavaScript, we have two more handles to add. These belong to the modal and allow us to
manipulate the title and image. Add the following `ids` to the modal:

```
<div class="modal fade" role="dialog" id="LightBoxModal"
aria-hidden="true">
    <div class="modal-dialog modal-lg" role="document">
        <div class="modal-content">
            <div class="modal-header">
                <h5 class="modal-title" id="ImageTitle">
                Modal title</h5>
                <button type="button" class="close"
                data-dismiss="modal" aria-label="Close">
                    <span aria-hidden="true">&times;</
                    span>
                </button>
            </div>

            <div class="modal-body">
                <img class="img-thumbnail" id="
                ImageShowcase" />
            </div>
        </div>
    </div>
</div>
```

Now, open the `index.js` file and add the following code:

```
$( function( )
{
    $( ".thumbnailImage" ).click( function( )
    {
        var imageURL = $( this ).attr( 'src' );

        $( "#ImageShowcase" ).attr( 'src', imageURL );

        $( '#LightBoxModal' ).modal( 'show' );
    } );
} );
```

Let's go through the new code line by line:

- **Line 1** checks whether the thumbnail image is clicked; if so, it runs the next few lines of code
- **Line 3** retrieves the image URL of the thumbnail from the source attribute
- **Line 5** sets the modal image source URL to the image URL retrieved from the thumbnail
- **Line 7** shows the modal

 It is important to do all changes first, then show the modal. Otherwise, elements may quickly change while the modal is loaded, which isn't a very good user experience.

We will now dynamically retrieve the image URL and update the modal accordingly. You might be wondering where is the title update; I will leave that as an extra task for you.

With this, the fourth and final project has been completed. As always, experiment with the code to truly see what it does.

Summary

In this chapter, we finished the fourth and final project by implementing an awesome light box to showcase the gallery's images. This was the final chapter. Thank you for taking this journey with me through four amazing and wonderful projects. I enjoyed every moment of writing this book and also learned a lot myself. I hope to see you in my future work.

Index

9

9GAG
  URL 243

A

Android KitKat promotional homepage
  URL 54
Anthony designer
  URL 56
Arild Danielsen Photographer
  URL 260

B

base project
  HEADER.php snippet file, refactoring 136, 137
  index.css file, refactoring 135
  index.js file, refactoring 137
  index.php file, refactoring 136
  setting up 135
  unnecessary files, removing 135
bitmaps
  about 13
  versus vectors 13
blog examples
  about 129
  Gawker 131
  Johnny Cupcakes 133
  Microsoft News 132
  TechCrunch 130
  Tesco Living 134
blog home page section
  carousel indicators, using 147, 148
  image slider, implementing 138
  implementing 138
  view 138
blog post page examples

about 159
Gawker 161
Johnny Cupcakes 163
Microsoft News 162
TechCrunch 160
Tesco Living 164
blog post page
  banner image, adding 167
  body, adding 172, 174, 175, 176
  contents 165
  extending 186
  implementing 166
  main content, implementing 167
  popular sidebar, contents 166
  post content 165
  recommended sidebar, contents 166
  snapshot paragraph, adding 170, 171
  title, adding 167
  useful links 177
blog posts
  cards, adding 152, 153, 154, 156, 157
  implementing 150
Bootstrap components
  about 34
  reference link 34
Bootstrap project example
  abstraction 44, 45, 46
  creating 42, 43
  footer, extending 48, 49, 50
  header, extending 46, 47, 48
  main body, extending 51
Bootstrap's grid system
  about 20
  basics 21
  column offsetting 33
  conclusion 34
  differently sized columns 25

differently sized columns with screen size
   restrictions 26
equal width columns example 23
examples 22
horizontal alignment 32
matching 27, 29
mixing 27, 29
multi-row, equal-width columns example 24
multi-row, equal-width columns without example
   25
usage 22
vertical alignment 30, 31
Bootstrap
   about 17
   history 17
   need for 19
   using 18
breakpoints 10
Bueno
   URL 113
buttons
   reference link 125

C

card component
   reference link 151
carousel indicators
   captioning 149, 150
   reference link 150
   using 147, 148
choice screening
   URL 116
Cloudinary
   URL 96
colors, Bootstrap
   reference link 105
column offsetting 33
common issues, website
   about 82
   navigation bar button anchoring issue 82
   navigation bar height issue 82
contact form
   adding 121, 122, 124, 125, 127
Contact Us examples, for single page websites
   about 111

Bueno 113
choice screening 116
design museum 115
Richman 112
this also 114
Contact Us section
   anchoring, to navigation bar 120, 121
   contact form, adding 121, 122, 124, 125, 127
   container, creating 117, 119, 120
   contents 117
   implementing 117
Content Delivery Network (CDN) 42, 96

D

Dan Kennedy
   URL 258
design museum
   URL 115
development environment
   prerequisites 41

F

Facebook
   about 188, 206
   URL 188, 206
Font Awesome
   about 194
   URL 194

G

Gawker
   URL 131, 161
generic reusable single page section
   implementing 90
   Our Team section container, creating 92
   reference link 91
   team member info text 105, 106, 107
   team member social links 107, 109, 110
   Team section, anchoring to navigation bar 93
   Team section, contents 91, 92
   team's pictures, adding 95, 96, 98, 100, 103,
      104
GIPHY
   URL 245
GoldSquare

URL 55
Google Photos
  URL 244, 257
Google+
  about 189, 207
  URL 189, 207

I

image slider
  back buttons, adding 143, 145, 146
  creating 138, 139, 141, 143
  forward buttons, adding 143, 145, 146
  implementing 138
image
  adding, to modal 266, 267, 269
introduction section
  anchoring, to navigation bar 70, 72
  creating 57
  current button selected, modifying 80, 81, 82
  header, placing on top 78, 80
  implementing 57
  jumbotron 59
  navigation bar anchor, animating 72, 73, 74, 76, 77

J

Johnny Cupcakes
  URL 133, 163
jQuery
  about 19
  reference link 75
jumbotron
  about 58, 59
  creating, with banner image 227, 231
  image, adding to 61, 62, 63, 65
  implementing 59, 60, 226
  large cards, implementing 237, 239
  overlay text, adding 232
  small cards, implementing 234, 236
  text and images, combining 66, 67, 68, 69, 70

L

light box examples
  about 255
  Arild Danielsen Photographer 260

Dan Kennedy 258
  Google Photos 257
  Pinterest 256
  Salter 259
light box
  contents 261
  image, adding to modal 266, 267, 269
  implementing 261
  modal, adding 261, 263, 264, 265
  modal, content appear dynamically 269, 271

M

Medium
  about 210
  URL 210
Microsoft News
  URL 132, 162
Minds
  about 191
  URL 191
modal
  about 261
  adding 261, 263, 264, 265
  content, appear dynamically 269, 271
  image, adding to 266, 267, 269
  reference link 266
Myspace
  about 192
  URL 192

N

navigation bar anchor
  animating 72, 73, 74, 76, 77
  footer visibility, fixing 77, 78
  location problem, fixing 77, 78
navigation bar
  Contact Us section, anchoring to 120
  section, anchoring to 70, 72
  Team section, anchoring to 93
navigation
  Contact Us section, anchoring to 121

O

overlay text
  adding 232

P

pagination
  about 251
  adding 251
  reference link 254
photo gallery home page
  contents 247
photo gallery home page examples
  9GAG 243
  about 241
  GIPHY 245
  Google Photos 244
  Pinterest 242
  vent 246
picture thumbnails
  adding 248
Pinterest
  URL 242, 256
popular sidebar
  contents 166
principles, responsive design
  about 9
  bitmaps, versus vectors 13
  breakpoints 10
  desktop-first 12
  maximum values 11
  minimum values 11
  mobile-first 12
  nested objects 12
  relative units 11
  responsive design, versus adaptive schemes 9

R

recommended sidebar
  contents 166
refactored project
  reference link 137
relative units 11
responsive columns 14
responsive grid system
  columns 20
  rows 20
responsive grids 14
Responsive Web Design

about 8, 17
reference link 42
reusable project template
  about 37, 39, 40
  benefits 40
  Bootstrap project example 42
  creating 42
Richman
  URL 57, 113

S

Safari
  reference link 106
Salter
  URL 259
sidebar
  implementing 179, 180, 182, 184, 185
single page sections
  about us 88
  contact form 86
  examples 86
  opening times 90
  projects/work 89
  reference link 87, 88, 90
  usage 86
single-page website
  about 53
  Android KitKat promotional homepage 54
  Anthony designer 56
  different sections 85
  examples 54
  GoldSquare 55
  Richman 57
social network profile examples 225
social network sidebar examples
  about 187
  Facebook 188
  Google+ 189
  Minds 191
  Myspace 192
  YouTube 190
social network sidebar
  burger button, implementing 193
  contents 193
  implementing 193

reference link 193
sidebar CSS side, implementing 198, 203
sidebar HTML side, implementing 196, 198
social network timeline examples
  about 205
  Facebook 206
  Google+ 207
  Medium 210
  Twitter 209
  YouTube 208
social network timeline
  contents 211
  extending 223
  feed section, implementing 213
  implementing 211
  input section, implementing 212
  main body, adding 220
  post's timestamp, adding 219
  user's name/username, adding 218
  user's thumbnail image, adding 216
social network user page
  contents 226

T

TechCrunch
  URL 130, 160
Tesco Living
  URL 134, 164
this also
  URL 114

thumbnails
  home page title, adding 247
  implementing 247
  pagination, adding 251
  picture thumbnails, adding 248
troubleshooting
  about 52
  CSS not applying 52
  PHP errors 52
Twitter Blueprint 18
Twitter
  about 209
  URL 209

V

vectors
  about 13
  versus bitmaps 13
vent
  URL 246

X

XAMPP
  about 42
  reference link 42

Y

YouTube
  about 190, 208
  URL 190, 208

CPSIA information can be obtained
at www.ICGtesting.com
Printed in the USA
LVHW021155110822
725647LV00001B/24

9 781787 287068